Advice From Experience To New Real Estate Investors

Honest, Thoughtful, Real World Advice To Get Started And Grow A Successful Real Estate Investing Business

By: Kevin Perk

Smarterlandlording.com

Cover Image by misterfarmer from Pixabay

Dedication

To my wonderful wife

Table Of Contents

Introduction vii

Section 1 - Why Real Estate Investing?..1

Because Real Estate Investing Is Fun!...2

Because Real Estate Investing Gives You All Five!......................................5

Because You Have Been Bitten By The Entrepreneur Bug 11

Because Real Estate Investing Lets You Choose Your Own Rules 14

Because Real Estate Investing Provides A Cushion In An Ever Changing World
....18

Because Real Estate Investing Will Change Your Life For The Better...............21

Section 2 – What New Real Estate Investors Need To Know 25

The First Step Is To Fill Your Brain 27

What Newbies Need To Understand About Real Estate Investing 31

So, You Are Looking To Get Started 37

Your Frame Of Mind Is Going To Change. Go With It..............................42

Don't Wait To Buy Real Estate, Buy Real Estate And Wait 48

Don't Make These Newbie Mistakes 50

Even A Newbie Can Compete With Experienced Investors 57

What Type Of Property Makes A Good First Investment? 60

What Newbies Should Know *Before* They Become A Landlord 65

No Money or Experience? No Problem. Here Is What You Need To Do.....71

What Newbies (And Seasoned Investors) Simply Must Master 75

What Should A Newbie Real Estate Investor Be Cautious Of?................79

Section 3 – Buying Your First Property 85

iv

Questions You Should Ask Yourself Before You Buy Your First Rental Property 86

Preparing to Buy Your First Investment Property—Getting Your Own House In Order 91

Motivation Is The Key 95

It Is Best To Deal With The Property Owner "If" You Can 98

Putting The Numbers Together On Your First Buy And Hold Deal 101

Buyer Beware 107

Making Your Offer 110

My Offer Was Accepted! Now What? 115

Section 4 – Introductory Real Estate Investing Business Tips 119

Putting The Pieces Together —What It Takes To Be A Successful Landlord 120

Going From A Full-time Job To Full-Time Investor 124

How To Manage Your New Found Time 128

Avoiding Fraud: How To Steer Clear Of Being Taken 132

The Biggest Problem Real Estate Investors Have 137

Should You Incorporate Right Away? 139

Section 5 – Going Forward As A Full-time Real Estate Investor 145

How To Stay Afloat When You Feel You Are Being Pulled Under 146

Be Thankful 150

Dealing With The Pervasive Anti-Landlord Mentality 152

You Are No Longer Normal 155

About Kevin Perk 159

Introduction

Thank you for purchasing this book!

I wrote this book because I want to show everyone, from my own experience, that real estate investing really can set you free. I want to show that real estate investing really can provide you with all you want and more.

I designed this book for the "newbie." What is a newbie? A newbie is a person who is still learning about real estate and not yet made their first deal. It is also the person who has perhaps made their first one or two purchases but is still learning the ropes. If you are already an experienced real estate investor, this book will still be useful as a refresher and perhaps you will nod your head in agreement with many of the points I make.

This book is a collection of my personal "advice from experience." It is not some grand blueprint nor is it a step by step guide. If that is what you are looking for, you are not going to find it here. In fact, I am not sure you can find it anywhere because I really do not think it exists, even though many will claim that it does. The world of real estate investing is so vast, with so many different properties and markets, and so many different ways to go about it that there cannot be a one size fits all blueprint for everyone. Instead, I believe that real estate investors should listen to a variety of different advice and select methods that will best work for them and their situation. This book, therefore, will provide you with some generic advice to help guide you as you move forward.

This book is **not** a get rich quick book. I do not try to fill your head with dreams of sitting on the beach sipping margaritas while your real estate investments magically inflate your bank account. In fact, I will tell you again and again that real estate investing is a business that will require effort and work on your part. Sure, there are "home runs" in the real estate investing business, but they will be few and far between. I have hit home runs, but I have also struck out. I have, however, hit a lot more singles and doubles that eventually led me to home plate.

I want you to get to first base in real estate investing. From there, I want you to keep hitting and continue to grow. Dreams are a great thing to have and can be great motivators (mine was to get out of my nine-to-five job) and I want you to have some. It is not my intention, however, to sell you one with this book. It is my intention to provide you with reality-based advice that may help you achieve your dreams. There is a difference.

This book is also for the person who is looking to start off small, get their feet wet and then build their base of knowledge and experience. I am speaking to the individual proprietor (and their significant other) who want to learn the nuts and bolts, get their hands dirty sometimes, and manage their own properties. This book is for the person that is going to take an active role in managing their properties and building their business from the ground up.

I designed this book to provide advice in five different sections. The first describes why I think real estate investing is one of the best ways to change your life for the better. Not only will I tell you why real estate investing is fun, but I will also go through the many benefits, both financial and personal, that you will reap from becoming a real estate investor. I hope this first section will help you determine if real estate investing is the right thing for you.

The second section delves into what someone new to real estate investing needs to know. There is so much to know that there is no way that it can be covered in one book. What I can do, however, is draw from my own experience and point you towards small goals to get you started and get you thinking in the right way. In doing so I examine several of the mistakes that I and other real estate investors have made to hopefully keep you from doing the same.

The third section is an important one. I provide advice on buying your first investment property. I guide you through the right questions to ask, both of yourself and everyone else. I generally work as a landlord, so that is where most of my advice will come from.

Once you have done your first couple of deals, you need to move on towards getting your business growing and that is where I take you in the fourth section. The real estate investing business can be wieldy and things can easily slip through your fingers. Nobody wants things to slip away, so I discuss how to be effective and how to manage your time while working towards becoming your own boss and taking more control of your life.

In the last section, I provide some thoughts on going forward in this real estate journey. I tell you about some of the trials and tribulations you are likely to experience and what to do as you are facing them.

There is a lot of advice from experience in this book, but I need to say that I am not an attorney nor am I an accountant. I am simply a real estate investor with years of experience. You must and should seek your own competent legal and accounting advice before you undertake any major purchase or decision.

That said, thanks again for your purchase and support. Please keep reading and learning at Smarterlandlording.com and let me know how you are doing. I would appreciate hearing from you.

Section 1 - Why Real Estate Investing?

Why would anyone want to get into real estate investing?

There are a lot of reasons why and this book, specifically this first section, will describe some of them. I hope it will also help you determine if real estate investing is right for you. Truth be told, real estate investing is not for everybody. I have witnessed more than one person get very excited about becoming an investor, only to later find out that it was not exactly what they thought it would be. There is no problem with that nor is there any reason to be upset. We all have different strengths and attributes and it is best to know if real estate investing is the right thing for you *before* you get in. There are a lot of dollars involved in real estate as most real estate does not come very cheap. Serious money can be spent very quickly, and before you do that it is best to know if it is the right thing for you.

I think real estate investing is fun and provides some of the best financial benefits possible. I also believe it will change your life for the better. Read through the next few chapters and see if you might agree with me. If not, that is okay. If so, I think you will have been bitten by that entrepreneurial real estate bug and be well on your way towards achieving some of the best that life has to offer.

Because Real Estate Investing Is Fun!

Here is the idea I want to start you off with. **Real estate investing is fun**! I want to start here because having *fun* is important. When something is fun, it becomes something that you want to do, something you look forward to. If something is fun you are going to keep doing it. Doing something fun will leave you feeling much more fulfilled and satisfied. I am a prime example. I have been doing this for 15 years now and I still think it is fun! I have fun with real estate almost every day.

Not everything that you will do in your real estate investing career will be fun, as there are negative parts to everything. As a whole, however, I think you will enjoy it. Why? Real estate investing is so broad and so diverse and there are so many ways to do it that it can be tailored to what you like, and who you are. That is one of the wonderful things about real estate.

What exactly is so much fun about real estate investing? A lot of things come to mind, but in order to be brief, six things stick out in my mind as especially fun about real estate investing.

1. **Hunting For Properties** – Do you enjoy watching house hunting shows on TV? Do you like going to open houses? I do, too. It is like you get to be a bit of a spy into people's private lives. I do that just about every day. I am always out and about looking at properties. Big properties, little properties, perfect properties, abandoned properties, it does not matter. Every property is unique and lets you see how people really live, both good and bad. Plus, just when you think that you have seen it all, the next property you look at will amaze and/or baffle you. You just never know what you will see at your next property. And that is what makes it so fun and interesting.

2. **Playing With The Numbers** – After hunting for properties, I like to get the brain going and play with the numbers. I like to try and determine if the property is actually going to be a good deal for me or

2

figure out what I can do to make it a good deal. Yes, I might already have a basic answer before I even visit the property, but putting everything together in a spreadsheet helps me collect my thoughts and makes things begin to look real. That is both fun and exciting to me. Section 3 of this book will help you with the fun of putting all of the numbers together

3. **Putting The Deal Together** – A lot of folks may think I am crazy here (perhaps I am just a bit), but it is fun trying to put all of the pieces of a deal together. The money, the repairs, the people, the offer, the closing are all both trying **and** fun. I was scared of this part of the business when I first started out. But with just a little education and experience it became fun to make offers and see what worked. Putting the deal together really gives you the opportunity to be creative and solve problems. You learn quickly that everything is negotiable. It is very challenging, but to me being challenged is part of the fun.

4. **Making Old Buildings New Again** – Ever since I was a kid, I have always liked old buildings. The creaking, the unique features, and the history all enthrall me. What happened here? Who lived here? How can I make this property better? These are all fun questions for me. Watching an old, worn out building come to life again is really one of the best things about the business for me. And since I live in a historic area full of old buildings, I get the added benefit of fixing up my city. It is such a pleasure to drive around and see the properties that I brought back or renovated being used again. Sure, with any renovation or rehab you will run into unexpected problems, but to me that is just more fun as I try to solve them.

5. **Providing Quality Homes** – There are several phrases that are just wonderful to hear. These include "What a beautiful home." or "It is so nice to live here." Hearing someone say that and more to you can really make real estate investing worthwhile.

3

6. **Teaching Others About Real Estate Investing** – I have always had the heart of a teacher. In fact, I have taught introductory college geography courses for over 25 years. I enjoy watching faces light up when people "get it." I think it is fun to watch students put the knowledge they have gained from me to work and make it on their own. It is my way of giving back and to me, it is more than fun. *It is rewarding.*

You may not think that the six things I just described here about real estate will be fun for you. That is okay. Real estate is so diverse and there are so many ways to do it, that you will likely find something about it that is fun for you.

Do you like to work with your hands?
You can do that in real estate.

Do you like to work with numbers and figures?
You can do that in real estate.

Are you good at investigating, or do you want to learn how to be?
You can do that in real estate.

Do you like designing things such as an addition to a property or perhaps an entire building or even computer programs to help you find properties?
You can do that in real estate.

There is no single, correct way to be a real estate investor. Any way you choose that makes you happy and is fun (so long as it is ethical and legal, too) is a good way to go.

Because Real Estate Investing Gives You All Five!

Did you know that there are five ways that you can earn a return, or financially benefit, from an investment? Not just real estate investments, but any type of investment. These are:

- Cash flow or Rate of Return
- Federal Tax Benefits
- Leverage of Other People's Money (OPM)
- Principal Paydown
- Appreciation

Let's go through an example of buying stock in the Tesla car company to demonstrate how these five financial benefits work.

If Tesla pays out a dividend on each share you own, that would be cash flow or rate of return.

If you got a tax break from Uncle Sam or your state, such as a tax credit, for each share you bought from Tesla, that would be an example of a tax benefit.

If you could borrow money from someone and invest it in Tesla stock and then sell that stock for a profit, that would be leveraging other people's money.

If you bought Tesla stock with OPM, held it, and paid back the principal (likely with some interest in there as well) over time, that would be principal paydown.

Appreciation comes into play if your Tesla stock increases in value while you own it.

However, here is the thing: how likely is it that Uncle Sam is going to give you a break for buying stocks (knowing Tesla they might)? How likely is it that you can walk into your bank and ask for a loan to invest in the stock market? How likely is it that Tesla stock will go up or down in value? Will the Tesla stock pay dividends or not?

Who knows? Who knows if you will even get one of these benefits?

With real estate you will be much more likely to get all five! Real estate is the **only investment** that I know of that potentially gives you *all five* of these types of return. That gives real estate a heck of an advantage!

Think about it. What other investment product out there gives you the flexibility and possibility of so many types of returns like real estate does?

Let's take a look at each type of return in a little bit more detail and discuss how real estate investing can provide it for you.

1. **Cash Flow** – Cash flow is profit and it is how I make a living. Simply put, cash flow is income less expenses. It is what you have remaining after you pay all of the real estate-related bills. To illustrate, think about a rental house from which you might collect $1,000 per month in rent. Let's say your monthly mortgage payment on that house is $500, your taxes are another $200 and insurance is another $50. Let's also say that over the course of a year your maintenance costs average another $100 per month. Add all that up and you have total monthly expenses of $850. That leaves a monthly cash flow, or profit, of $150 per month or *$1,800 per year*. Now, think about owning ten more rental properties. Think about owning a 50-unit apartment building where each unit provides $150 cash flow per month. When you do, you begin to see just how great this type of return can be, how it can lead to financial freedom, and why investors love it.

    Cash Flow is, in my opinion, the most important thing to think about with any real estate investment. There are all kinds of metrics out there that people throw around all of the time, such as *cap rate* or *cash on cash return.* You can calculate those if you want, but I have never used them in my real estate investing career, and you do not have to either. At the end of the day, we just need to know how much we are going to get paid. Do not let investor lingo scare you off. Keep it simple and focus on cash flow.

2. **Federal Tax Benefits** – There are three Federal Tax benefits that you can receive from owning real estate.

    First, the Federal Government wants you (the private market) to provide housing for others. In order to help you do that they came up with a tax benefit called *depreciation*. Depreciation is an amazing thing. Depreciation allows you to deduct a portion of your property's value from your income.

    How? The Internal Revenue Service has decided that residential real estate bought for investment purposes has a shelf life of 27.5 years. If you buy an investment property where the building is worth $100,000 (land does not really have a shelf life as it lasts forever), you can deduct over $3,600 (about 1/27.5) off of your income—**for almost 30 years**. Depreciation is a wonderful benefit that can really add up. Imagine now having 10 of these properties. The total deduction to your income every year from depreciation would be about $36,000.

    Secondly, if you own rental properties, rental income is considered passive income by the IRS (although owning real estate is in no way passive). The IRS does not treat all income the same. The income you get from your nine-to-five job is considered active income. Active income is taxed differently. It is subject to social security taxes, for example. Passive real estate rental income is not subject to these taxes. This means that you do not have to give about 7.5% of your paycheck to Uncle Sam. That extra income goes into your pocket.

Finally, as a new real estate business owner, you can deduct all sorts of business expenses from your income, expenses that you could not deduct before. These deductions could include a home office, your cell phone, mileage, office supplies, etc. There are rules with these, so consult someone with more tax knowledge than I have. My job here is to just let you know about them.

Want to reduce your tax burden, get yourself some rental properties, and get started in real estate? There is no other investment that will do all of this for you.

3. **Leverage Other People's Money (OPM)** – Very few folks have enough cash saved up to buy real estate outright. If you do that is great— use it—but you do not have to. In fact, it is much more common to use other people's money to do it. How? By getting a loan or a mortgage to purchase investment properties, and then having your tenants pay it back as a part of their rent payment to you. Plus, the amount of time you have to pay OPM back can be as long as 30 years. No other investment gives you this benefit. You can even structure your purchases and loans so that none of your own money is actually invested. It can all be OPM! No matter how you structure your real estate deal, you will receive this financial benefit. Can you buy gold or stocks with a 30 year fixed rate loan? No, you cannot. There is no other investment that has this great benefit. In fact, there is no other country in the world that offers the ability to do this. As far as I know, the United States is the only country to offer 30-year, fixed-rate loans. Use that benefit!

4. **Principal Paydown** – Using other people's money does not come without a cost. You have to pay it back with interest. With each payment you make you pay back a bit of principal, as well as the interest. With each payment, you are paying the loan down (unless you are paying interest only, which I generally do not recommend). With

every payment you make you are building equity and getting closer and closer to owning the property free and clear. With every payment you make, you are building wealth and it is fun to watch your net worth rise month after month just by paying your bills.

5. **Appreciation** – We know that real estate prices do not always go up. In fact, many got burned in the real estate crash that occurred a few years ago. Why did they get burned? Because they were looking for short term gains. They were looking for the quick buck. There is nothing wrong with that, and sometimes you can make a quick buck with real estate. The real money in real estate is in the long term. Over the long term, real estate is likely going to go up in value. What do I mean by long term? I mean 15, 20 even 30 or more years. After every downturn or crash, prices eventually rebound. Perhaps not quite as exuberantly as they did before, but with the Federal Reserve constantly pumping money into the system, real estate values will rise over time. Don't believe me? Take a look at this chart from the United States Federal Reserve showing the overall supply of money in the United States.

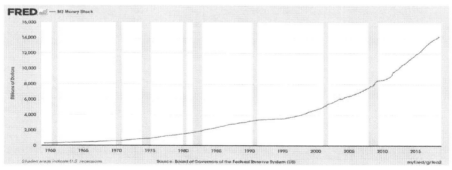

This chart depicts a nice, steady, long-term trend up. You can ride this long term trend by owning real estate. Real estate is a hard and tangible asset. They are not making any more of it and everyone needs a place to live. If you choose wisely, real estate can protect you from shocks to the system.

Have I convinced you to buy real estate yet? If this short summary of the five financial benefits of owning real estate does not do it, I do not know what will. I simply do not know of another investment that gives you all five of these benefits. What other investment provides an income by using other people's money, while giving tax breaks, and increasing the balance sheet, all while hedging against inflation? *Only real estate investing does.* What a deal it can be!

Because You Have Been Bitten By The Entrepreneur Bug

You may not yet realize that becoming a real estate investor also makes you an entrepreneur. You will be starting and running your own business! Yours, not someone else's! This is a huge step and congratulations to you for even thinking about taking it! Most people will not get as far as you have. Understand however, that being an entrepreneur means change: changes to you and your life. Becoming and being an entrepreneur is like having a compulsion or picking up some kind of bug. When caught, it works on you day and night. It becomes a sort of obsession. You will not be able to wait to get started because you will begin to realize just how powerful a tool real estate is and how much it can change things for the better.

Done right, real estate investing will lead you down a wonderful new track in life. Not only can real estate investing give you back your time that you are now giving to your employer, but it can also open up many new doors and present many new opportunities. Real estate investing can lead you down paths you might never have been aware of or even considered before.

How does real estate open those doors?

By thinking and learning about becoming a real estate investor, you begin to leave the nine-to-five, clock in and clock out, paycheck mentality behind. Your mind moves beyond those things. You begin to enter into the entrepreneurial world, and once you enter it, there really is no turning back. Entering the entrepreneurial world is like nothing else. It can be very exciting, sometimes mind-blowing and often scary. It is like your eyes have suddenly been opened and now you see the world in a completely different way. When this happens to you, and it will, you will have caught the entrepreneur's bug. Don't try to kill this bug. It is not a bug that you want to get a shot for and get rid of. **Let it take over.**

Entrepreneurs are a different type of person. They have to be. You will become a different person too. The main thing that makes entrepreneurs different from others is that they have learned to take risks. Most people are scared to death of taking risks. Entrepreneurs, on the other hand, have learned how to look for and find places where a potential profit can be made. They seek risk. They have learned how to put a deal together, and then work hard as hell to make sure everything comes out alright. And when everything works out well, the feeling can be exhilarating! You cannot wait to get back out there and wash, rinse and repeat. As you progress in your entrepreneurial career you learn from your mistakes. You will learn from others, and you will learn from your competition. This learning makes you better and it makes you stronger. You tweak, improve, refine. Hopefully, you start putting money in the bank. Hopefully, you have great success from catching this bug.

It is hard for people to catch the entrepreneurial bug. If it were easy, most people would be entrepreneurs, but they are not. The nine-to-five paycheck path is, for the most part, tried and true. It presents much less risk and offers a lot more comfort. It is where most are guided, and what they are taught to do. I was. Comfort is appealing and it is easy, most will take this easy path.

Does working a nine-to-five really provide comfort and security? Not really. Layoffs happen all the time and *without warning*. You really have no control over what the higher-ups who give you your paycheck are doing, and they could be really messing up or worse. You need something that offers you protection. You need something that offers a backup plan. Becoming a real estate entrepreneur can offer those things.

To those of you that have caught this bug, I offer a word of caution. Be wary. Its bite and the success it brings can cause blindness. It can blind you into potential pitfalls. It can trick you into thinking that if you can be successful at one thing, you can be successful at all things. The bug can make you think that perhaps a Christmas tree farm, a used car lot, a snow cone stand or even a roofing or contracting company (these are all true stories, by the way) are good investments to start. Some of these ideas may very well work, but many will not. They all, however, will shift your focus from the thing that got you where you are, **real estate investing**. Try not to forget what got you here in the first place, real estate investing. Be careful of shifting your focus away from the hand that feeds you.

Because Real Estate Investing Lets You Choose Your Own Rules

You just read about the tremendous financial benefits of becoming a real estate investor and about becoming an entrepreneur. Real estate can and will change your life in so many ways. But, on top of everything that I have discussed so far, perhaps the best thing about becoming a real estate investor is that real estate investing allows you to *create your own rules*.

What do I mean by that?

Let's think about it. If you currently work in a typical nine-to-five job, someone else is generally making all of the rules. What rules am I talking about? Basic rules that you might not have even considered before. These rules range from when you have to get up in the morning, who you have to work and interact with, when you get to go home, when and how long you can take off, how much your labor is worth. This list could go on and on.

These rules will no longer apply to you as a real estate investor. Because real estate investing is such a diverse profession with so many variants and possibilities, it lends itself to being one of the few techniques that the average person can actually use and develop to gain more control over their lives. By being able to set our own rules, real estate investors really do achieve a level of freedom that I do not think many others achieve. After some education and a little bit of experience, a real estate investor can almost write their own program to satisfy whatever it is that they want to do.

What rules will you be able to choose by becoming a real estate investor? There are many but here are the rules that are the most important.

1. **Choosing Real Estate Investments That Work For You** – Real estate is not a one-size-fits-all investment strategy. Unlike investing in the stock market, there are all kinds of ways to invest in real estate and

different types of real estate to invest in. There are single-family houses and apartment buildings. There is raw land and there are industrial buildings. There are triple net strip commercial buildings and mobile home parks. You get to choose what fits you and your needs best. It could be only one or it could be all of them. It is up to you. No one is going to tell you to draw up an offer on an apartment building and have it on their desk by noon on Thursday. You choose the rules about what you want to invest in and when you want to invest in it. You are in charge and no one can tell you to do otherwise.

2. **Developing Your Own Real Estate Investing Program** – There are numerous real estate investing strategies out there. I'm a landlord. I chose the "buy and hold" strategy. But there are plenty of others. You can buy, fix and flip (actually, I do this strategy as well when an opportunity presents itself). You can find properties for other investors by wholesaling or being a bird dog. You can learn to develop raw land. You could learn to repurpose old buildings. Or you could do a little of each one. It depends on you and what you want to do. Whatever you decide to do, you get to choose the rules. You can look for opportunities wherever you think they might be.

3. **The Location Of Your Investments Is Up To You** – The world, as they say, is your oyster as far as real estate goes. You can invest wherever you desire. Do you want to stay close to home? You can. Do you want to invest near the mountains or the beach? You can. Do you want to be a turnkey investor and invest in properties where I live in Memphis Tennessee? You can do that also. Do you prefer urban, suburban or rural properties? Those are out there waiting for you, as well. Want to do a little bit of it all for diversity's sake? You can do that, too. The limitations on where you choose to invest are few. The location you choose is totally up to you and your capabilities.

15

4. **Your Lifestyle Is Your Choice** – I hated going to my nine-to-five job. It just did not fit me at all, as I have never really been a morning person. I like to work nights. I still do work, but I do it on my own schedule now. If that nine-to-five schedule you are used to works well for you, then there is no need to change. If you would rather only work early in the mornings or late into the evenings, you can do that, too. No one will be there telling you when to punch in and punch out.

    Is it a nice day outside? Go take a walk. Feel like sleeping in? Go ahead. Want to get that deal worked out today? Get to it. It is all up to you. You choose.

    The 40-hour work week is gone, too, if you want it to be. My goal was to work less. If you want to work 80 hours a week, feel free. You can work as little or as much as you want in your real estate investing business. It is completely up to you. The lifestyle you choose for yourself is up to you. No one else will set the rules for you. Punching in and out is for the other guy.

5. **You Choose The Money You Want To Use** – One thing I have learned from experience is that the money is out there. Money for a good deal is rarely a problem. It is truly amazing how many sources of money are out there for real estate investors. Do not think that banks are your only source of funding. There are plenty of other sources including private lenders, hard money lenders, and owner financing. You can even potentially use your own IRA retirement funds and you can, of course, use your own money. You really are only limited by your own creativity and eagerness.

    Do you only feel comfortable using a local bank? That is fine. Don't like the fees of certain private lenders? Don't use them. It is up to you. You can choose your own rules here as well. One of the best choices, in my experience, is to find and use private lenders. Private lenders are just what they sound like. They are people with money looking for a decent return. They are people that you can actually talk to and work together with on various deals that regular banks may never touch. Try doing that with stocks or with some other type of business.

6. **You Choose Who You Want To Work With** – As a real estate investor you can (almost) be demanding about who you wish to work with. Remember that you bring significant resources to the table as an investor and therefore you get to choose at least some of the rules in any transaction. Many think that those who have the money make the rules, but that is only partially true. Money is only one part of the puzzle because the person with the money needs the deal and the expertise you are offering just as much as you need them. What is more, your boss will no longer be able to force you to work with people who are incompetent or that you do not like. You will get to choose. This does not mean that incompetent and dislikable people will not be in your circle, but you will now have the power to say no to them.

Would you like to choose your own rules? Of course you would, that is why you are reading this book. Real estate investing will let you choose them. It may be a little tough at first and you will stumble around a bit trying to figure out your new rules and routine, but you will get the hang of it eventually. Plus, the rules you choose will not be fixed in stone. You can change the rules as your business grows and develops. You can change the rules as market conditions change. And you can change the rules simply because you want to. Any way you look at it, your ability to choose how you want to live and run your life will be greatly expanded by becoming a real estate investor.

Because Real Estate Investing Provides A Cushion In An Ever Changing World

Change is inevitable. No matter how much we want things to stay the same, they will not. Everything will eventually change. Some changes occur slowly over time and can be processed and absorbed. Getting older comes to mind. Other changes are thrust upon us very suddenly and without warning. They can cause great upheavals in our lives. Imagine what the loss of a job would mean, or perhaps a sudden illness or even a collapse in the stock market.

These sudden changes are usually things that are out of our control. You cannot control how the large company you work for is managed. You cannot control how well the stock market performs. The best you can do is to provide yourself with cushions for these shocks to the system. Real estate investing is one thing that provides an excellent cushion. Real estate investing provides for **more** control over both your personal and financial life, which means more cushion for unexpected changes. In fact, once you get into real estate investing, you may even begin to embrace change.

Here is what I mean.

Think about life at a regular full-time job. You get up every day, commute to work, get assigned tasks, complete those tasks and collect a paycheck. You might get a bit of vacation and some sick leave, perhaps even a 401k with an employer match. Do you have any control over what time you can arrive or leave? Do you have any control over what tasks you are given? What about who you work with?

You do in real estate. You could just quit your nine-to-five, but that would be a big shock to the system, and then what would you do? You still have to eat and keep a roof over your head.

You could also line up another job, perhaps even move to another city entirely. Would you end up in the same place you were before? They say the grass often looks greener for a reason.

What if you got laid off without any warning? What then? What is your backup plan?

Real estate investing provides you with that backup plan.

A bit of imagination will help you see how.

Imagine having 10 rental properties generating $200 per month *cash flow*. That is $200 left over after all expenses are paid. That is $2,000 per month or $24,000 per year. Now imagine that the worst happened (at your day job) and you got laid off. Could you at least live off of the cash flow while you sort things out? True, you may have to downsize your budget and pinch pennies, but $2,000 per month is a much better cushion than $0.

Now imagine that you have 20 rental properties generating $200 per month cash flow. $4,000 per month or $48,000 per year is not too bad. Remember, cash flow is what is left over after all expenses, such as the mortgage, insurance, and repairs for the property have been paid. That $4,000 per month is pure profit for you to live on. Could you think about going without your full-time job now? Imagine what that cushion would feel like. There is no feeling like not having to care about a nine-to-five job anymore.

Imagine not having to get up at the same time every day. Imagine not having a commute. Imagine having your lunch in the park if you wanted to, or just taking the day off because you felt like it or had a cold. Your properties are still cash-flowing. Even in your sleep, your properties are cash-flowing and working for you. I can think of no better cushion than that.

Now imagine that you have all of your time back. Imagine that you are able to use that time to focus on real estate investing. Imagine using that time to focus on growing your own business. Your focus allows you to expand to 30, 40, 100, 200 properties. You are able to hire people to help you. Would you still worry about being laid off or when your next report was due? Would you sleep much better at night? Would you feel like you had more control over your life?

I am not saying that real estate investing will make everything in your life perfect. You will still face changes and challenges as things will still break, contractors will disappear without notice, deals may be lost and tenants will be tenants. But you will have more control over these events because you have taken back more control of your life. The cushion that real estate investing will provide for you is a great thing to land on.

Because Real Estate Investing Will Change Your Life For The Better

You are reading this book for a reason. You feel like something needed to change. Perhaps you feel like you need more income. Or perhaps, like me, you really just wanted to be in more control of your time and thus your life. Whatever the reason, it all gets back to the feeling you have that something needs to change, and change for the better. Real estate investing can change your life for the better. It can provide all of the things you dream about. It can also provide a whole lot more.

Have you ever read the book <u>Rich Dad, Poor Dad</u> by Robert Kiyosaki? If not, I highly recommend it. It changed the way I look at things and it will for you, too. For those of you who have not read it, the book describes a kid with a "poor" dad and a mentor he called his "rich" dad. Poor dad was an educator who believed that wealth is gained by acquiring more and more formal education. Rich dad, on the other hand, was a businessperson, who understood the power of real estate investing.

At the time I read the book, I immediately identified myself as the "poor" dad. I had gone to college for over eight years. I have two master's degrees and was considering getting a Ph.D. I felt that I had to keep getting more and more certificates in order to justify more and more income. In all honesty, I liked being insulated from the real world and being in school. That was because I had not yet learned how it worked, and no one in college was really going to teach me.

Kiyosaki's book helped set me on the path towards a better life with real estate investing and I hope this one will do the same for you. Do I regret my time spent in school? Maybe a little, and I still would like to perhaps get a Ph.D. one day. But I would do it for me, because I want to learn, not because I think it will increase my pay. See the difference? I have the time and the money to do these things now, on my own terms. I bet you are looking for the same sort of ability.

Real estate investing gave me that ability. It gave me the ability to live my life on my own terms. And while I would tell you to be cautious with anything labeled by Kiyosaki more recently, as he sold his brand (maybe he should have talked to his "rich dad" again before doing so), his original advice in his first book still holds true. Real estate is a powerful life changing tool but you have to learn how to use it, and it is going to take a bit of effort on your part.

In the remainder of this book I want to outline many of the things that you will need to know as you go forward. I want to help you begin to understand where to put your focus and lead you down the path towards finding out if real estate investing is right for you and which way you should go with it.

I want you to understand what real estate investing is before getting too involved, and I want you to learn from my experience. Everything I am writing about in this book is true. I have seen it or done it, succeeded or failed. I may repeat myself from time to time but that is only because what I have to say needs repeating. If you take away anything from reading this book, take away this: *real estate investing can make you successful and give you everything you have dreamed about.* It will take learning, work, and effort on your part. If you are okay with that, then let's go forward and take a look at some of the things that you will need to know.

Section 2 – What New Real Estate Investors Need To Know

When beginning any large task it can be hard for one to know exactly where and how to start. After all, newbies do not know what they do not know! Real estate investing is no exception and there is much to know. The knowledge is not locked away somewhere, hidden in libraries and inaccessible behind a paywall; it is right here, in front of you now. It is also out there in a myriad of other places. The knowledge can be found in books, in blogs, and even in videos and podcasts.

What someone starting out should do is to bite off a little bit of that knowledge at a time. How much is a little? How long will it take? Those items will depend on you. If you try to bite off too much at once it will become overwhelming. Once something becomes overwhelming, most people stop and give up. To avoid getting overwhelmed, I suggest that those starting out learn the basics first. One can specialize later on as they discover the aspects of real estate investing that appeal to them. Everyone has different sets of skills and differing amounts of resources. Find out what fits you and then full speed ahead.

Learning how to be a successful real estate investor takes time and is not something that should be attempted overnight. It took me over a year of studying real estate investing techniques before I bought my first investment property. I'm still studying and learning today.

Unfortunately, you will hear the exact opposite. There are plenty of people out there who will try to sell you on how easy real estate investing is and how quickly it can be accomplished. While some may find real estate investing easy and quick, most do not. Learning anything new just takes time. So, let's take some time and discuss what it is you need to know to get started.

This section is designed to help you as you begin your real estate investing journey. You have already made the decision to go forward, now you have to figure out how to do just that. My aim in this section is to get you thinking about where it is that you want to go with real estate investing, what you will have to do to get there, plus some things that you should avoid.

The First Step Is To Fill Your Brain

Congrats! You have begun your journey towards financial freedom and getting more control over your life. You have gotten over the first hurdle, researched various real estate investing techniques, and decided to get into it. You will be glad you did because I think that real estate investing is one of the most interesting and satisfying ventures you can start.

If you are like me when I started, real estate investing is completely new to you. Don't worry about that, as you can and *will* learn. It will be a bit overwhelming at first, but let that excitement you feel right now carry you through.

I felt just as overwhelmed as you likely feel right now. There is so much to learn and so much to do! How can it all be accomplished? Believe me, it can and will get done. But for now, the first step; the first thing you need to do is fill your brain with real estate investing knowledge. How? These five tips will get you started.

1. **Read Everything You Can On Real Estate Investing** – Read books, newspapers, and magazines. Read whatever you can about real estate. It does not matter what type of real estate is being written about or how big or small the project is. You need to read it all. You need to learn real estate terms, concepts, and business models. Seeing them on paper will help you. Reading about real-world examples will help you. Reading all of this material will also help you decide what parts of real estate investing are best for you.

2. **Listen To Real Estate Podcasts** – The great thing about podcasts is that you can listen to them anywhere. You can listen to them while driving, cleaning the house, or whatever. Plus, there are so many that are filled with great information (The SmarterLandlording Podcast is one of the best, in my humble opinion). Podcasts allow you to use what would otherwise be downtime to learn.

3. **Scan Business Sections And Magazines** – Even though most articles will not be about real estate investing, they will be about business, other forms of investing, entrepreneurs, taxes, etc. Remember that you are becoming an entrepreneur. By reading about business you can learn a lot about business terms and concepts, how business people think and what they watch for. I, for example, subscribe to and read the Wall Street Journal and several other business magazines like Inc. and Money. Over time, your brain will begin to absorb what you read and you will begin to apply what you are learning to not only your new business, but your everyday life as well.

4. **Subscribe To Various Real Estate Websites** – When I was getting started there was nowhere near the content on the internet that there is now. Today there is a ton of great content out there, so much so that it also can be overwhelming. I would suggest picking a few select websites that you can always refer back to and sticking with those. Otherwise, it can all just be too much. A word of caution is needed here. There are some not-so-good sites out there, which only sell dreams and want your money. Be very cautious and dubious of any site promising that you will be "drinking champagne on the beach in no time," or asking for a lot of money upfront, or guaranteeing you "elite" information. They are only selling a dream and trying to scam you. Seek out good solid information from solid investors. As you fill your head with more and more real estate investing knowledge, you will be able to tell the good from the bad.

5. **Attend And Participate In Business Oriented Meetings** – Face to face contact is still essential. Local knowledge just cannot be beaten. I would strongly suggest you investigate if there is a local REIA group in your area. REIA stands for *Real Estate Investors Association* and these associations are filled with other local investors, many of whom are like you and just starting out. There could also be numerous other business organizations where you can go and network with other like-minded

people and make contacts. If you live near a college or university, they often offer free business-related lectures. Go and listen. Take full advantage of any type of offering to meet and mingle with other business people. For example, we have a weekly real estate investors' lunch that anyone is free to attend. I have learned more at those meetings than almost anywhere else. Don't have a real estate group near you? Start one with Facebook or Meetup. Cultivate the connections you make as they can grow into very resourceful friendships. Be sure to participate. Do not just stand against the wall. Do not wait to be asked to dance. Get out there and meet people.

Yes, starting out is overwhelming but you have already taken the first steps. Keep going! The items above are mentioned because I want you to fill your brain with the thoughts and concepts that will enable you to be successful. Filling your brain is the first step. You have to learn to think like a real estate investor and to do that you have to study and network with other investors.

It is unfortunate that very little about investing or business is taught in formal education. In fact, you often have to re-educate and retrain yourself. Think about it. Did you come out of high school or college with a "pro or con" attitude towards business? Be honest with yourself and then ask why. How many business courses were even offered at your school? Were any of your teachers business owners? Had they ever ventured outside of the nine-to-five world to develop a product, sell it and make a payroll? Some of your teachers may have had a bit of entrepreneurial experience, but I think it would be safe to say most did not. I would even bet that most of your teachers had little if any exposure to the business world and business people. Thus, your teachers taught what they knew from their own experience or what they read in books and believed to be true. Their teachings lacked business acumen.

Retraining yourself can be done. It will take a little time and effort, but before you know it, you begin to see and think differently about the world. Your new knowledge will be working for you.

What Newbies Need To Understand About Real Estate Investing

Even after 15 years of experience, I still try to make time every month to get to my local REIA meetings. I even serve on the board of directors to try and help the organization, because it helped me so much when I got started. These REIAs can be found in almost every major city in the US and if you, as a newbie or even a more experienced investor, have not found one yet, I highly recommend you do so. As I said, I still go to mine for several reasons. One is that I usually learn a thing or two that will help my business. Second, I get to network with others in the real estate investing biz to talk shop or just vent. Finally, I get to meet a lot of newbies who are at their first meeting.

With newbies, I can often see the excitement in their eyes. They are excited because they have found an arena filled with so many other like-minded people. This find provides them with confirmation of their ideas. This real estate thing is real! Their minds are swirling with the thoughts of the millions of dollars they are going to make and they are ready to jump in. The thing is these newbies do not realize just how much they do not know. They do not understand just how much there is to understand.

Because I have been active in my local REIA and have written about real estate investing for a while now, I often get recognized by or introduced to these newbies. Newbies always do what anyone new to something always does. They ask a series of rapid-fire questions. They want to know how I got started, how many units I own, how this and how that, etc, etc, etc. I usually try to answer their questions and I enjoy the look of excitement they often have (I wonder if I had it once?). To be completely honest, in answering their questions I also try to rain on their parade a bit. Not because I'm a jerk, but because it needs to be done.

Why? Because newbies just do not realize how much they do not know. As someone who wants everyone to be successful, I know that the truth needs to be told before they get too far in. There are downsides to this business and they need to hear about it. Now. If they do not hear about any of the downsides, when it hits them they will become disillusioned and then likely quit or fail.

I do not want them, or you, to fail. So let me rain on your parade a bit while you still have that excitement in your eyes, and tell you several things newbies need to understand about real estate investing before going in.

1.   **There Is Going To Be Some Work Involved** – Yes, work! Just like anything else worth having, real estate investing is going to take work. It can be fun work but work nonetheless. You have to work at being successful at real estate investing. I have seen so many people get sucked in by infomercials, by HGTV, by traveling bands of "gurus" holding one-day seminars in major cities and by "here today gone tomorrow" folks on YouTube and elsewhere. These are the "drama and dream" sellers.

You know the ones I am talking about. They only show the investor sitting on a beach, or at the job site with perfect hair and clothes and just focus on the drama. They offer no real information until you buy into the "higher levels." These dream sellers are designed to take your money or hook you on the drama. To prove my point, I was once contacted by an HGTV producer. After speaking to her for a while it was obvious that she was more concerned with creating drama than actually showing what it is I do and helping others to learn about it. There is nothing wrong with dreams or creating drama for entertainment, but it is not okay to try and sell that as reality. The reality is not going to be found on TV. Instead, the reality comes from understanding that achieving your dreams can be done with real estate investing, but that it will take work.

Real estate investing can and will make you rich, but the chances of becoming magically rich overnight are slim. There is nothing wrong with having a goal of living at the beach but if you think you can simply forget about things and ride the waves all day, you are mistaken.

I want you to know that real estate investing is a business and running a business takes work. Not so much working with your hands, like painting or sanding floors (though it can be). Rather it takes brain work. It takes keeping the investing business going and growing. It means putting out the fires, finding new income streams, buying and selling, learning new techniques, setting up and refining systems, and so on and so on. I'm sorry, but there is no magic formula to get out of work. Real estate investing can be highly rewarding work; it can also be work that you will find fun and that you <u>want</u> to do.

2. **Success Will Not Happen Overnight** – Becoming a successful real estate investor does not happen overnight. The belief that it can happen overnight is often part of that dream being sold by those I described above. Sure it is possible to hit a home run your first time at bat, but it is unlikely. You need to practice a lot before you can hit consistent home runs. Honestly, you are much more likely to strike out or hit a few singles while you are learning the game.

Success as a real estate investor is also an ongoing process. Sure, some people will advance further and faster than others, but that is true with everything about the human condition. Remember, though, that becoming successful and quitting your nine-to-five job can be done. I am proof of that. It did not come overnight however, and your successes likely will not either.

3. **There Is A Lot To Learn** – Imagine that someone has asked you to design an app for mobile phones from scratch. Could you do it? Unless you already are skilled in designing apps the answer is likely no. To develop a new app you would need to gain certain knowledge and

skills. You would need to start climbing that learning curve. Climbing that curve means reading up on programming and app design, watching YouTube videos from other designers, possibly enrolling in school or attending weekend seminars to network and discuss options with other programmers. Eventually, you would be able to develop something, in perhaps six months or a year. Your success would depend on how well you topped the learning curve.

The same scenario is true for real estate investing. When meeting newbies I often tell them to think about starting out as if they were going back to school. There will be a lot of material to digest. You may and should attend a lot of seminars and networking events. You may even spend a bit of money on a real estate course or two. There is a lot to learn. Newbies simply do not yet grasp all of the things they have to learn about. These can include real estate pricing, rental rates, rehab costs, financing, insurance, tenant screening, marketing, who is buying, who is selling, where to invest, where not to invest, and on and on and on. How long will it take before you learn enough and can do your first deal? Depends on how quickly you can get above the curve, but it is unlikely it will not happen overnight.

4. **Real Estate Investing Might Not Be For You** – Over the years I have found that real estate investing is not for everyone. I have watched a lot of people come into the business and eventually leave. They like the "dream" part, but they do not like the "work" part, that goes with it. Or, they may simply prefer focusing their time and resources towards another goal. Some will discover they are just not cut out for it. Others will discover that they like or prefer the security of the nine-to-five job. There is nothing wrong with any of that. The fact is you might not like real estate investing, so I suggest you just dip your toe into the real estate investing waters first. Would you buy a car without driving it? No, you would take it for a test drive to see if you like it. Do not go without a real estate test drive either. Perhaps

purchase one single-family house before you buy that apartment building. It can be a lot more difficult and expensive to sell unwanted property than it was to buy it in the first place.

5. **Is Your Spouse or Significant Other On Board?** – All of the greatest ideas in the world can come to a dead stop if your partner or spouse is not on board. Your dreams will never come true if your life partner says no. Trust me; if you decide to go forward without your significant other, you are in for some very rough times indeed. Becoming a full-time real estate investor is a radical step for most, and many will simply not understand why you are doing it. You must get them involved in your dreams and journey from the very outset, from the very moment you have the idea that real estate investing is where you want to take your life. They may not see your vision at first. They may not get why you want to leave the comfort and protection of your nine-to-five job. They may need to get won over to your way of thinking. I highly encourage folks to bring their spouses to their local Real Estate Investor Association meetings and get them involved in their plans. Let them read the same books and listen to the same podcasts you are. After all, two heads are better than one and the last thing you really want is to be in a position of having to choose between real estate and your significant other.

6. **Not Everyone Is Going To Share Or Understand Your Vision** – When you first discover real estate investing, it is exciting. You want to tell the world about it. You want to share your excitement and perhaps get other people you know on board. Be ready. Most are not going to understand what you are doing and some will even try to dissuade you from going forward. This discussion will come from family and friends and even from people who know you the best. It will be very disappointing and disheartening and it can be deflating. They will tell you that you are crazy. They will tell you horror stories and anecdotes of every bad thing they have ever heard about real

estate and real estate investing. My advice in such a situation is this: unless the people you are talking with are real estate investors or entrepreneurs, try your best to put what they say aside. Realize that their experience is only in the nine-to-five world. A world that you are trying to leave. On the other hand, listen to and take advice from those who have achieved what you wish to achieve.

Raining on parades is no fun, especially newbie real estate parades. I hate to dampen the excitement. But, experience has taught me that a little rain is a good thing. In order to be successful, newbies need to know and think about the six items I have discussed above before they get in too deep. By understanding what they are getting into and knowing that they will have to study and work hard, newbies will have some of their dreams fulfilled by real estate investing. That beach house may very well be within reach.

So, You Are Looking To Get Started

The real estate investors association that I belong to provides a host of opportunities for investors to meet and network. These opportunities range from formal presentations to informal lunches. Newbies often come to these meetings and eagerly soak up all of the information they can get. Some of these newbies will make their way to me or other experienced investors to introduce themselves and ask for help. These introductions are often led off with "Hello, I'm looking to get started in real estate investing." The questions just keep coming from there.

Often, several of the more experienced investors at the meeting will sit around and try and answer some of these newbies' questions. Most of us have heard their questions before. In fact, their questions are probably the same ones we asked at some point early in our careers.

So what do we tell these newbies? Where does the discussion go when they tell us they are looking to get started?

The first thing we often do is share many of our successes and failures, especially the big ones. We are at a point in our careers where we can now look back with pride when things worked out or laugh at what was once a horrible situation. These stories are always good for a few chuckles and some shock value. They also help the newbies feel more comfortable and at ease, as these stories demonstrate that everyone has ups and downs but made it through. Then we get down to business and try to point people in the right direction. We give advice from experience, even though it may not be what they want to hear or what they are expecting.

1. **It Is Going To Be Hard** – This, point blank, is often the first thing we tell them. Real estate investing, despite what you may have heard somewhere on YouTube or at another seminar is tough. Just like anything else worth doing, it will take effort on your part. We emphasize this point often because there are so many out there who

try to claim otherwise. We want you to be cautious and to keep a discerning eye out as you go on this journey.

2. **You Do Not Need To Incorporate** – I find so many newbie investors are quite focused on forming an LLC. They are rightly concerned about liability and lawsuits. I get that. Here is the thing: you do not need to incorporate at first. You do not need an LLC when you are starting out. You just do not have the liability yet. What you need to do is get out there and get started and an LLC is not necessary for this. Put your time, focus and money towards other things. Yes, asset protection is important but insurance will do for now. LLCs and other corporate structures can always be added as your business grows

3. **There Is Much To Learn About Real Estate Investing** – Real estate investing is a broad and wide-ranging field. There are many strategies and techniques that will help you get to where you want to be. You will need a broad understanding of the field at first, and then you need to learn a little about yourself and what you want to do. All of that takes time. And depending on where you are starting from, you can have a rather steep learning curve. It has never been easier to learn. Reading materials, podcasts and videos can be taken almost anywhere at any time. Use your time wisely and learn all you can.

4. **There Is No Need To Spend A Lot Of Money On A Real Estate Education** – Yes, you have a lot to learn, but you do not have to spend thousands to learn it, especially some of the basics. A lot of basic information is out there for free or very little cost. Plus you can also learn a lot just by networking and talking to other investors. Ask one or two out for lunch and you will be amazed by what you can learn in an hour. If, after getting a basic understanding of general real estate investing fundamentals, you wish to focus on a particular aspect then, by all means invest in a course that you truly feel will help you

advance your goals. I and many others I know have made similar investments. Just take heed and be wary of those who are up-selling or wanting you to pay to join higher and higher level groups. They want your money more than they want to help you. The up-selling rarely ever stops until you are out of money. Pay for a course once and be done.

5. **Just Start Somewhere** – You cannot possibly learn everything there is to know about real estate investing and at some point you just need to get started. To get started, focus on a few types of real estate in a few areas. Learn what those properties sell for, what they rent for and what the market is like in those areas. Become a specialist by starting in a particular area. By doing so, you will be able to know if a potential deal is presenting itself. You can always expand or move on to other areas later if you choose.

6. **The Deals Are Out There** – The market may be high, or it may be bottomed out. Either way, there are deals out there, you just have to learn how to find and acquire them.

7. **No One Is An Island** – Networking with other investors is important. You will need and want their help as you go through your real estate investing journey. You will need help on your journey from lawyers, accountants, contractors, and others. Sharing ideas and deals with other investors will also be a key to your success. Having lists of potential buyers and sellers of real estate is also extremely helpful. You simply are going to need other people. Get out there and meet them. Ask people what they do for a living and what they are looking for. Figure out how you can help them and they will help you.

8. **The Money Will Find You** – Money makes its way to truly good real estate deals. That may be hard for you to believe, but it is true. Do not worry so much about finding the money, instead spend your time learning what a deal is, how to find them, and how to secure them.

Then use your network of people that you have developed, so you have someone to bring that deal to. If you have the knowledge and the network, you will be amazed at how easily deals, without a lot of money on your part, can be made.

9. **Keep Coming Back** – There is only so much we <u>can</u> tell you at our first meeting together. Honestly, there is also only so much that we <u>will</u> tell you at our first meeting together. So keep coming back. Get to know us. As we get to know you, we will share more and more with you. We do not mind sharing because there are so many deals out there. We like helping other people and know that there is plenty of real estate for everyone.

10. **We Want To Help** – Believe it or not, we do. It is one of the main reasons that we go to these investor meetings. We like to help folks who are starting out. Why? Because someone once took the time to help us get started and it is now time for us to return the favor. Like I said above, keep coming back and get to know us. We really do want to help you be successful.

It often happens after such a short meeting with such a huge amount of information that there are naturally more questions and perhaps a sense of overwhelming confusion. If you feel this way right now, try not to worry about it as we have all been there and felt it before. Go and keep reading, listening or watching. Spend your time wisely. You are basically back in school now, real estate school. This time it is of your own choosing. No one forced you to go. You want to be in school because you can see the benefits ahead.

I guess we scare some people off because we never see them again. That is probably for the best. They should hear it now before they get in too deep. But if after talking to us you still think this real estate thing is right for you then keep going. One day you will be the one speaking with the voice of experience.

Your Frame Of Mind Is Going To Change. Go With It

Catching the real estate investing bug changed everything. I sort of knew that it would, but I did not realize how much. I knew, for example, that I would have a lot to learn before I ever made my first purchase, and learn I did. I knew I would have success and disappointment, and I hoped that my lifestyle and the track I was on would change as well. They did.

What was not expected was a change in how I viewed the world. As I became more experienced, I began to think about and see the world in ways I had not before. My frame of mind, or my established way of thinking about things, changed. Not in a bad way, but in a way that helped me be successful. If you want to be successful, your frame of mind will change, and likely need to change, as well.

What changed and how did it help me? Let me start at the beginning.

I went to school like most people did. I studied somewhat hard and then I got a job. I was pretty good at what I did and advanced in my field. I worked a typical nine-to-five job with weekends and holidays off and two weeks of vacation per year. I thought I had learned quite a bit. I felt pretty sure I knew what life was about and how the world worked. In fact I did know a lot; unfortunately, I knew a lot about being in the rat race.

Real estate investing opened my eyes. I quickly became aware of how much I did not know and **had not** learned in all that time. I realized that the world is a very different place than I thought it was.

Perhaps you have a similar story. I hope to get you on the road towards changing your frame of mind a bit quicker than I did, and help you become more successful faster. Below are five changes that I want you to begin thinking about. I want you to keep these five items in mind as you go about your daily routine. I want you to start seeing the world in a different way. I want you to start thinking like a real estate investor rather than a wage earner.

When reading through the changes I describe below, you might just recognize yourself and how you currently view the business and real estate investing world. If so, do not worry too much it. You are just realizing that you need to change. Change takes time. If you stick with the real estate investing bug, change will come.

1. **Taking A Risk Is Both Necessary And Rewarding** – My education and the first jobs I held taught me that risk is a bad thing, that risk was something to be avoided. They both reinforced in me the idea that you did not want to be the one that stuck their head out there, as it could (and would) get chopped off. This was especially true of the government jobs I worked in, where anything risky was strictly taboo. Those motivational posters on the wall did not reference the squeaky wheel getting the grease; rather they depicted a nail sticking up and getting hammered down.

    While the mantra that risk was bad was not explicitly taught, it was subtly enforced over the years. Recall your school years where you learn not to stand out because those that do often get punished or ridiculed. You learn to just follow the rules, keep your head down and pass the test. In life we often see risk-takers get hurt or go bankrupt. The message is constantly reinforced that risk is bad.

    The truth is that we, as humans, would not be where we are if it were not for risk-takers. Yes, some got hurt, killed, or bankrupted along the way but many more succeeded and we are all better off for it. These success stories are what you now need to find and focus on.

    Becoming a real estate investor will involve risk. There will always be risk. There is risk by going into business. There is risk in buying a vacant building. There is risk working with contractors. There is risk with tenants. The trick is to learn how to take a calculated and managed risk rather than just bumbling into something. And learning how to take a calculated risk can be done. Learn to embrace some risk, at least some calculated risk. It is this calculated risk that will make you successful.

2. **Change Is Necessary** – Just as most people are against taking risks, most are also against change. Nothing good comes from change, or so they believe. It is best to keep things the way they are. Most educators and government agencies are not going to promote change either. Stay the course, study hard and get a good job and you will be fine.

Think back in your life. How many times in the past have you ever asked or wondered why something was done in a certain way, especially if it seemed like there was a better way? How many times did you hear the answer "It has always been done this way"? Or perhaps you heard something along the lines of "If it isn't broke, don't fix it." I know I heard it many times and the reason is that people do not like change. I never liked when my questions about change were glossed over. Real estate investing had a great appeal to me because asking why and seeking change are considered natural. To be successful in real estate investing, one has to find the path no one has taken before. One has to accept and embrace change

3. **It Is Okay To Make Money** – If you are like me, you grew up with limited means. You could not have everything you wanted and you coveted the things that others had. You may have even thought that it was wrong for some to have so much more than you. You may have thought that wealthy people are greedy, and since greed is bad, wealth is bad.

Hogwash!

Wealth, as long as it is not stolen, is not bad. Nor is the desire for it, or for the better things in life. That desire is perfectly natural. It spurs us on to provide things to our fellow humans that they desire. Think about it. Everybody wants a decent place to live. Everyone wants to better their position. There is nothing wrong with you taking action and making some money if you are able to provide something that someone else wants. The more you provide, the better off you, your tenants and everyone in general will be.

We have to be careful with this "wealth is bad" attitude, as it seems to be becoming a bit more pervasive. Is it any wonder? How many of you were taught this attitude in school? Think back to your American history courses. Were the rich of the late 19th century providing their fellow humans with better and cheaper goods and services or were they "robber barons?" I know what I was taught. Few, if any, of my teachers understood that the wealth I build today rehabilitates my neighborhood and city, employs many people and allows me to expand my business and give back more. Think about all of the good you could do if you had more to give. Wealth is not bad. Some *people* are, but wealth is not.

4. **Businesses Are Not Bad Either** – Business cannot survive unless they offer a product or service that people freely want. The best businesses do that well, and offer lots of people lots of things that they want. People can freely choose not to do business with someone, and if enough people choose this path, that business will go extinct. Thus, successful businesses actually work hard to attract and maintain customers. It is their lifeblood. They have to offer a product that someone wants. If a business decides to charge too much, or acts like a jerk, we often take our business elsewhere.

You have done this before and I have as well. We have all had bad service or been ripped off in the past. Think about those businesses that did this to you, are they still around? Perhaps they are, perhaps not. If they are, I bet they changed some of their practices over the years.

You need to learn this lesson. That being good at or successful in business is not bad. Instead, it is something that should be strived for. As a real estate investor you will need to provide a product that people willingly want to purchase from you. If you do not, you will fail. It is that simple. You will need to work hard at providing a quality service at a decent price. You have to make the majority of people you serve want to be a repeat customer and that can be very difficult. Nothing else guarantees success.

5. **Entrepreneurs Are People I Should Watch More** – How many times have you watched a famous entrepreneur and thought they were just not quite grounded in reality? Perhaps after reading this, you have an idea why. It is because they think so differently from the rest of us.

    Entrepreneurs are unique people. They often see things that others do not. In my early dealings with entrepreneurs I just did not understand them and thought they had a screw loose. So I avoided them. I should have done exactly the opposite. I should have hung around them to learn what made them tick. To learn and perhaps understand how they came up with all of their ideas. Today I know better. I like to hang around entrepreneurs. Their ideas and actions are invigorating. I try to surround myself with entrepreneurs as much as possible. You should as well. There is nothing better to help get you thinking differently and focused on making you, your life and your business (and therefore your community) better.

So there you have it. Changes to my frame of mind and the way I think have I believe made me a better and more successful real estate investor. How much of yourself did you see? Do not worry too much if you saw a lot, as people can and do change.

These changes generally will not come overnight. Instead, these changes are developed over time as you learn more, experience more, and meet and interact with new people. So, get out there and seek out successful people you want to emulate. Take them to lunch. Get to know them. Join your local real estate investors association. But first and foremost, get started investing. It will truly open your eyes!

Don't Wait To Buy Real Estate, Buy Real Estate And Wait

I know. The title of this chapter sounds like a hokey saying. Hokey or not, the saying is true. Anytime is a good time to buy real estate and there is no better time than now. It does not matter if the market is up or down, sideways or flat. Anytime is a great time to buy. Sure, there can be real estate bubbles and times you should not follow the crowd. Bubble or not, the trick is knowing what to buy and what not to buy no matter what the market conditions are.

Real estate is a great investment. It is solid and tangible. You can see it. You can go stand on it. Most of it is not going anywhere, nor is much more being made. Real estate, no matter where we are in the business cycle, is always wise to buy. But, you have to buy wisely.

So how do you know what to buy and what to avoid? How do you know what to buy when the real estate market is red hot and everyone else is in a buying frenzy?

There are three things to keep in mind.

The first thing to keep in mind is that **numbers never lie, ever**. The numbers on a piece of real estate will tell you if it is a good deal or not. If you run the cash flow analysis described in other sections of this book and the numbers are favorable, buy. If they are not, walk away or re-negotiate. Be honest with yourself. Do not try to make the numbers fit to make it work. If the numbers do not fit, walk away from it.

The second is that **cash flow is king**. If you have good cash flow, then everything else is gravy. With positive cash flow your mortgage will still get paid. Positive cash flow will ensure that your taxes will get paid. It will ensure that your other expenses will, also. Plus you will still have some cash left over to put food on your table and gas in your car. Sure, a downturn could put a crimp in things, but if you have good cash flow in the beginning you should be okay no matter what cycle of real estate investing market you are in.

The third thing to keep in mind is to **never bet on appreciation**. What is appreciation? It is an increase in the value of the real estate over what you paid for it. If you are betting on appreciation then you are *speculating*, not investing. There is a difference and you need to be aware of it. There is nothing wrong with speculating. It has its place. Speculation and speculators can be hit hard and be hit fast. Speculators are usually the first to fall in any real estate crisis.

Speculators bet on the quick rise in real estate value. We learned back in 2008 that real estate will not necessarily keep going up in value. When things get going hot again, this fact is often quickly forgotten and exuberance rules the day. You do not want to be the last person holding a speculative piece of real estate when the music finally stops.

You might ask yourself how you can possibly find anything to buy when the real estate market is hot. The low hanging fruit will be gone and everyone has to work harder to find good deals, but the deals will still be out there. Even in hot real estate markets people still die, get divorced, change jobs, downsize, and do a host of other things that could potentially create the right deal for you.

Be patient. Remember the three things I mentioned above. Trust your numbers. Remember that positive cash flow is king and do not bet on appreciation. If you follow this advice you will be able to ride the real estate market waves with ease. You will be left standing after the next crash hits as it always, always does. You may in fact be in a great position to buy everyone else's mistakes at a serious discount.

Don't Make These Newbie Mistakes

Everyone was a newbie once. Depending on the type of project I take on, sometimes I feel like I still am. Newbies are newbies for one reason: they are new to real estate investing and thus lack experience. This lack of experience can often translate into newbie mistakes. These mistakes are just a part of the learning curve and we have all made them.

Mistakes from inexperience are, however, generally preventable. All one has to do is listen and learn from someone who has been there and done that. Absorb the knowledge and then endeavor not to repeat it.

One thing I have noticed as I speak with more and more people who are just getting started in real estate investing is that the same mistakes seem to pop up again and again. So much so that I began to keep track of them. I list them below. Read and learn.

Mistake #1: Not Properly Screening Tenants – Tenant screening is perhaps the most important thing a landlord does. I see too many newbies take the word of potential tenants and forgo the full background check, thinking it will save them time and/or money. Why do they make this mistake? It is because they most likely have been in a world where people keep their word, a world in which most people are not trying to scam you. Unfortunately, this world does not exist in landlording. You cannot trust anything that a potential tenant tells you. This does not mean you have to be ugly, but it does mean that you have to verify everything and screen everyone.

Mistake #2: Not Considering Their Real Estate Investments As A Business – Newbie real estate investors, while highly motivated, are often lacking in the business organization department. Of course newbies are disorganized; this may be their first go at a business. How to organize a business is something you have to learn. As a business person, you cannot treat real estate as a hobby. This is real life! You cannot commingle funds, lose receipts, and generally keep things unorganized. If you want to make money and be successful you have to treat real estate investing as a business. Otherwise, that money that comes in, if it comes in at all, will quickly disappear. Leaving you wondering what happened to it all.

Mistake #3: Falling For The Drama – Do you like drama? I hope so because as a real estate investor you are going to get a good dose of it. You will hear some of the best stories ever told. You will see and hear amazing performances from contractors, appraisers, bankers, and others. The drama will come at you in all shapes and sizes. Some of the stories may actually be true and some of the drama may be based in reality. But you know what? Their truthfulness or reality does not matter. Rent is still due when the rent is due, a contract is a contract, and I expect people to do what they say they will do. Being the nice person that you are, you may want to accept the drama. Do not do it! Think very carefully about this. Will your bank or lender let you slide? Will the grocery store? No, they will not and neither can you. Does it mean you will need to develop a thicker skin? Yes, it does.

Mistake #4: Doing Anything On A Handshake – Newbie real estate investors will often do a deal on a handshake. Why not? A handshake has worked well so far. I am here to tell you that it will not work now. It is amazing how quickly tenants can forget or how differently they will remember what was said. It is also amazing how quickly unscrupulous investors can take your deal away from you. If you do things with just a handshake, you are going to get burned. Yes, you can make payment arrangements or whatever if you want or need to, but insist that everything be put in writing.

Mistake #5: Not Understanding The Costs – How much does it cost to put carpet in a small living room and dining room? How about to paint the walls? How much does it cost to clear up a clogged toilet? What about keeping the grass cut? How about the fees to do an eviction or help you with your taxes? You have to understand what these costs are in order to run your business properly. It will take time for you to learn them all, but you need to at least know that they exist and will need to be paid. If you do not understand the costs of doing business, your money will quickly disappear.

Mistake #6: Not Understanding How The Law Applies – The days of being able to change the locks and turn off the lights if a tenant stops paying are long gone. In fact, if you did any of that today you might be the one that ends up in jail. There are a lot of rules and hoops that we real estate investors have to jump through today. And many of today's rule-makers flat out do not like nor do they understand real estate investors. Thus the deck can be stacked against us. Either way, you simply have to know what the laws are for your particular area.

Mistake #7: Never Taking A Look At Your Investments – Newbies often fall for the old adage that no news is good news. They often think that they can just sign the tenant up, hand over the keys, and then forget about things as long as they pay. Or they think that the property was purchased so cheaply that there is no way anything could go wrong. Nothing could be further from the truth. Tenants can do strange things, such as not tell you their boyfriend moved in, or that they got a dog, or that the sink has been leaking for months. Cheap properties are often cheap for a reason. Things can and will be hidden just beyond the newbie investor's sightline. As a real estate investor, you need to understand that someone has to go and check on the property every few months or so, even if you never hear from the tenant. Do not assume everything is okay. It may be, but it may very well not be and ignoring your property could cost you thousands later on. Dig deep; find out why something is so cheap and why you have not heard anything.

Mistake #8: Mixing Friends And Family With Your Business – Newbie real estate investors believe that their friends and family will make perfect tenants or partners, and they often make the mistake of working with and renting to them. After all, they think, what could be better than working with someone you know and trust? There is some truth to that statement and everything could go smoothly. But what if it does not? What if your friend or family member gets in a bind? Will they think they can stop paying you for a while, because after all, what are friends for? Trust me: this is exactly what they will think. The best way to avoid this situation is to not place yourself in it. In reality, renting to friends and family members is a terrible thing to do. Working and going into business with them could be as well. Money between friends and family can do very strange things. Think long and hard about it. If things happen to go south with your friend, are you ready to evict them? If not, how will you pay your bills? If so, what is going to happen to that friendship? There is no way to win this situation, so do not rent to friends and family in the first place and be very careful when working with them.

Mistake #9: Being Too Excited – Newbies are often overly excited to have discovered real estate investing. They should be excited as real estate investing can and will change lives. This excitement is electrifying and I remember it well. I was so excited to get into investing that I could not wait to get my first deal done. The problem is, this excitement, this great desire to get into the game, can cloud your judgment and make mediocre or bad deals appear to be good. Never ever think that you just have to "get one done" and that things will sort themselves out from there. Remember to trust your numbers; they are not lying to you. Rely on them and your intuition.

Mistake #10: Being Too Innocent – There is a very unfortunate part of this business, one that takes many newbies a while to learn. It is that you get to see a totally different side of people when dealing with tenants, contractors, and other investors. You get to see inside people's real lives, not just the facades they put on for everyone else. These dealings often leave us more experienced folks with a discerning eye and a somewhat thick skin because we have seen the "real thing" too often. People have to work hard to gain our trust. We lost our innocence a long time ago. We no longer assume on the front end that most are trustworthy. I hate to say it, but newbies are often just too innocent and trusting. They have not seen or experienced what we veteran real estate investors have. Unfortunately, newbies need to think that everyone is going to try to get into their pocket and pull one over on them. Of course, that is not true of everyone, but there are enough out there to make saying it here necessary. "Trust but verify" is a good rule to live by. Remember to get everything in writing and be very careful about who you give your money to. It can be very hard to impossible to get it back.

Mistake #11: Failing To Do Fundamental Research – Most people who are just starting out in real estate investing realize that they have to analyze the property numbers to find out if the potential purchase is a good deal. What they often do not understand is that there is a lot of background research that goes beyond the property numbers to understand if a deal is really a deal. The numbers on any individual piece of property can look fantastic, but what about the overall area that property is located in? What about the trends in real estate values or rental incomes for the location? There is a lot more to know than simply the one-percent rule, the maximum allowable offer (MAO), the fifty-percent rule, the loan to value (LTV), etc. There is a lot of fundamental background research that often needs to be done but is not. There is more to real estate investing that cannot be input into a simple formula.

Mistake #12: Forcing The Numbers To Work – Many new investors simply try to force the numbers to work. They try to force the property into being a deal. They hate losing the excitement of finding their first potential deal when the numbers say it does not work. It can be really deflating. You cannot let those feelings get in the way. The rent is the rent. The repairs are the repairs. The expenses are the expenses. The numbers are the numbers and no amount of massaging is going to make the numbers change. Do not try to massage. The numbers are not lying. If the numbers are saying no, they mean it.

Mistake #13: Underestimating Rehab Costs – I'll be honest, this is one that even experienced investors can have a tough time with. It is one that we all have to try and get a hold of because underestimating a rehab can quickly lead to a serious mistake. A newbie's best bet at understanding rehab costs when they are just starting out is to go simple. Find an easy patch and paint rehab. Learn from that experience and then move on to a more complex and bigger job. Otherwise, be sure to get estimates from trusted colleagues or contractors. Taking on a major rehab is a complex job that can quickly become overwhelming. Again, if the numbers do not work, or if you are just not confident on the costs, move on to the next deal.

Mistake #14: Thinking Real Estate Investing Will Be Easy – Real estate investing is often fun, but it is not easy. I am not going to sugarcoat it and lie and say that it is just so I can sell more books. There is no instant success model and you should be very cautious of anyone trying to tell you that there is. There is no one system, book, video, or course that will make real estate investing become easy. If you fall for the dream of easy, you will quickly get discouraged and end up losing the drive and excitement that got you here in the first place. Remember the old adage: if it were easy, then everyone would be doing it. Sure, buy some books, watch some videos, listen to podcasts and take a seminar or two, but tailor them to your own specific needs and circumstances.

I hope, the above discussion will keep you from making the same mistakes that I and many other investors made when we were starting out. Have I perfected things yet? No. I still make mistakes and will never stop. You will make them, too, no matter how hard you try or how smart you are. It is just a part of being human. You can, however, learn about them and thus possibly reduce the chance of making these mistakes. No matter where you are in your real estate investing career, the learning never stops. You have to keep learning to keep moving forward. The key is to learn from your mistakes and not make the same ones others have made. That key is what this chapter was all about.

Even A Newbie Can Compete With Experienced Investors

Those getting into real estate investing for the first time often believe that there is no way they can compete with more experienced investors. They believe that more experienced investors will find the deals before they can, that they will outbid them or just plain outsmart them. This viewpoint, while understandable, is quite wrong. It is a viewpoint that newbies need to change and change quickly if they want to have hope of success. If left unchanged, this viewpoint will lead to fear and this fear will then translate into inaction. In other words, this viewpoint will lead to failure.

Let me help you set things straight. You are wrong to think that you cannot compete with the more experienced investors. You can and you will compete.

Just think about it for a second. Everyone was a newbie at one time and everyone managed to compete and build up successful businesses, despite the fact that there were more experienced investors ahead of them.

Sure, the more experienced investors may have more business savvy and be way ahead of you in many ways *now*. But everybody had to start somewhere, and I bet they were thinking the same thing that you are when they were getting started. What if they had let their fear win?

There are several reasons why you can compete with more experienced real estate investors.

For one, there are just too many properties out there. All of these properties mean that there is too much potential for developing real estate deals. In Memphis, TN, alone (where I live and work) there are over 300,000 individual properties. Now multiply that across the country. Multiply that across the world. In all of that you will find one property that will work for you.

Second, all of these properties just lead to too many different deals. There is no way any one investor, group of investors, hedge fund or whatever can get them all. If they try, market forces will often push them back down, opening up a door for people like you.

Third, investors get tied up with their existing projects and therefore cannot have their eye on or get every potential property and every potential deal. An investor may, to give an example, purchase a small multi-family building that needs a significant rehab. That purchase and rehab will likely take that investor out of the picture for a while as they get the property fixed up, rented, and cash flowing. They may not have the resources to acquire and rehab another property at the same time. This situation will create an opportunity for someone else.

Fourth, investors get in or get out of the market all the time for a whole host of other reasons, again creating opportunity for you and other investors. Investors will move, get divorced, retire, get sick, or even go bust. No one gets out of this business alive and gets to keep things forever. A morbid thought for sure but all of these things create a fluid market and opportunities for the newbie investor.

Finally, other investors will make mistakes. They might have failed to learn the lesson about positive cash flow. They may take on a project they had no business taking on, or they may misread the market. I hate to hear about these stories and unfortunately have had some good friends go under. The fact remains that the world keeps turning and new opportunities are made, because people make mistakes every day.

These five points demonstrate the wonder that is the real estate market, or any market for that matter. Markets are always changing as everyone goes about their daily lives making thousands of individual decisions that no one person or computer model can ever hope to capture. The market is never static. It is too big and too fluid. This is why you can compete.

As a new investor you need to learn, to observe, and then get creative and find the opportunities. You might stumble or fail a few times, but eventually you will hit the mark before everyone else beats you to it.

What Type Of Property Makes A Good First Investment?

What type of property should you invest in first? Should you buy a house, a duplex, a tri-plex, or go big and go straight to apartment buildings and shopping centers? This question is very often one of the first that I get asked by newbie investors. This question is very difficult to answer because everyone is different as is every piece of property. People simply have different skills, aptitude, access to capital and goals. Each property, from single family homes to industrial parks, is going to have unique advantages and disadvantages and there is nothing inherently wrong with investing in one type of real estate versus another.

That said, in my experience, residential real estate is the easiest to get into and it has the least steep learning curve attached to it. So for the newbie real estate investor, I recommend residential real estate investment properties and that is what I am going to discuss in this chapter. There are three types of residential investment properties. These are: single family homes; the "plexes," as I call them; and apartment buildings. All three can be great investments but you need to be aware of the advantages and disadvantages of each one before deciding which is right for you.

Single Family Homes – Single family homes are properties with just one dwelling unit. They can be detached homes on acre lots or townhomes lined up in row. Even condos fall into this category. Single family homes can be great investments. The best feature of single family homes is that they generally are the only properties you can sell on the retail market. You often get a higher price when you decide to sell than you would with other types of residential properties. This feature often makes single family homes great properties for long term buy and holds, or flips.

You can make excellent cash flow with single family homes in many markets across the United States. Further, we investors can get some very favorable financing for single family investment properties. Rates are currently amazingly low as I am writing this in early 2019. Investors with W-2 (regular job) income and a good credit score can get loans with low fixed rates financed over 30 years, just like one receives with an owner-occupied house. There is no place else in the world where that can be done. Both pricing and loan rates make this type of investment property very attractive.

In many areas of the country, however, the price of a single family home will not permit positive cash flow. In other words, unless you are paying in cash for an expensive home or have a large down payment, the principal and interest payments on the amount you will have to finance will not generate positive cash flow. This is simply the way some markets operate, so choose wisely and run your numbers carefully.

A downside to single family investments is the fact that when your tenant moves out, your house is 100% vacant. That means no income. Vacancy is obviously a cash flow killer. Think about this: if you have a monthly cash flow of $150 per month on a home that rents for $900 per month and it remains vacant for just 30 days-just one month-you have just lost six months of cash flow profit.

Theft and vandalism can also be an issue due to vacancy. When a tenant moves and a property becomes vacant it can be an invitation to thieves and vandals. They know what to watch for and it is just an unfortunate part of this business.

The "Plexes" - Duplexes, Triplexes And Four-Plexes – The plexes are two, three, and four unit properties. They are smaller multi-unit properties. These also make great first time real estate investments. Their main advantage is that they will still produce income when one unit becomes vacant. Unlike single family properties, the plexes are rarely completely vacant, so they are always likely producing income.

Another advantage the plexes offer the newer investor is that they can often get the same great types of financing that was mentioned above with single family homes. This is because Freddie Mac and Fannie Mae, the U.S. government-backed buyers of these loans, treat these smaller multi-unit properties the same way they treat single family homes. Those low fixed rates and 30-year amortization (debt repayment) schedules are great benefits for the first-time investor.

Largely because of this financing benefit, these smaller multi-unit buildings can also possibly be sold to owner occupants on the retail market. The market for these properties is therefore a bit larger and more robust than it is for larger multi-family properties. They can often be sold to someone like me, perhaps. When I was beginning my investing career, I wanted to generate some extra income so I bought a duplex and lived in one side while I rented out the other. It was and is a great strategy to get started in real estate investing.

There are, however, potential tax consequences to owning plexes that you need to be aware of. In Tennessee where I invest, these smaller multi-family properties are taxed at a higher rate if they are <u>not</u> owner occupied. This is a significant added cost. Your state may or may not do the same thing. Be sure you understand how your properties are taxed in your location.

<u>Apartment Buildings</u> – Apartment buildings are properties that contain five or more dwelling units. These types of properties can be fantastic income producers. If you buy them right and increase the income they produce, they will serve you well. However, they can be more difficult to manage and can also be severe financial drains.

Management of these types of properties has to be strong or they can quickly get out of hand. Tenant issues and faulty maintenance can easily add up to a negative cash flow situation. Such a situation often quickly leads to a death spiral of bankruptcy and foreclosure. You might think that you can just hand this type of property over to a property management company. If you do not know how to manage your property, or how to manage the property management company, you will end up on the short end of the stick and likely in the same death spiral. I have seen this death spiral happen again and again. I actually look for properties caught up in this death spiral because they often can be a great buy.

Financing these properties is also much more complicated. Say goodbye to 30-year amortizations and lower interest rates that you can get with single-family homes and plexes. To purchase apartment buildings, you will most likely need to go to a local bank and get an officer's line of credit or commercial loan. These loans have significantly higher rates and much shorter terms. Often terms of five years or less. In this way apartments are very much like commercial or industrial properties. This financial aspect of investing in apartment buildings offers the newbie investors a whole new learning curve that they may not be prepared for.

Selling apartments can also be much more difficult. Think about it: who is going to buy these types of properties? Certainly not a retail buyer, but another investor who is going to be looking at the same cash flow numbers that you were looking at when you bought the property. In other words, that investor will be looking for a deal just like you were.

So let's go back to the question at the beginning of this chapter. What type of property should you buy if you are just starting out?

It again depends on the investor, but my answer would be to start with one of the plexes. These properties hold many advantages for the first-time investor. One, you can generally get decent, long-term financing. Second, vacancy is not as big of a problem as plexes will produce income over multiple units. Finally, the resale market is fairly good for these types of properties. These three factors help reduce the risk for you first-time investors. If these types of properties are not available where you live, then go for single-family homes in stable neighborhoods for many of the same reasons.

Whatever you decide to do, do get into real estate investing today. Make it a goal to buy one or two investment properties over the next year. The low rates and decent prices that are around in late 2018 and early 2019 may not be seen again for a long, long time.

What Newbies Should Know *Before* They Become A Landlord

Landlording is my primary real estate investing strategy. Yes, I also take the opportunity to do a retail flip and some other things as well. But, I still believe that the best strategy to develop long-term streams of income and wealth with real estate investing is to become a landlord. Being a landlord will, in part, provide you with the income you need to do all of those things you have been dreaming about. The cash flow that landlording provides will replace your nine-to-five income, getting you out of your job and rewarding you with some of the good things in life.

It is for these reasons that you should consider becoming a landlord as well. However, I do not want you to go in blind. As I lay out elsewhere in this book, real estate investing can be challenging and I want you to know what you are getting into before you get into it.

1. **Being A Landlord Means Being In Business** – A truer statement has never been said. Tenants are not going to magically deposit money into your bank account every month while you just lie on the beach. Sure, lying around at the beach can and should happen some of the time, but it cannot happen all of the time and anyone telling you anything different is just blowing smoke. Businesses do not run themselves. If you do not run your business, it will run you into the ground. Even if you somehow acquire hundreds of rental units you will still have the business of management or the business of managing the managers. Be wary of anyone who tells you differently.

   Choose who you listen to wisely. There are many "gurus" out there who do nothing but sell dreams (and charge a pretty penny as well). But, there are also many "gurus" out there selling and giving valuable information. Understand that being a landlord means being in business and that building a successful business requires work. The hope is that after a few years of work you will get to live the dream a bit. If you do it right and stay focused, you will.

2. **Having Some Cash Can Be Really Helpful** – Cash is king. Yes, you can get started in real estate investing with little or no cash, but at some point in your investing career, you will need some cash. Trust me. Work hard now to get your financial house in order and be careful about spending all of your hard-earned cash. You simply must put some cash away for a rainy day. Why? Because rain will fall. The AC condensers will get stolen and you will need money to replace them. The roof will start leaking and you will need money to repair it. If you do not make the repairs, your tenants will eventually leave, ultimately leading to a downward spiral that can be hard to pull out of. A bad property leads to bad tenants, which leads to no income, which leads to pain for you. Cash also gives you options and breathing space. When everything goes bad at once, have a bit of cash to fall back on will keep you sane. Remember what I said at the beginning of this paragraph, cash is king. Always keep some on hand.

3. **The Law** – The landlording business is shaped by law, and landlord/tenant law will determine so much of what you can and cannot do. It will dictate what your lease needs to say, what criteria you can or cannot use to screen tenants, what types of fees you can charge, how much those fees can be, and how you can get rid of a tenant when they stop paying. The law can stipulate much, much more and there is no standard set of laws. Every place is different from state to state and city to city. Ending up on the wrong side of the law can be very easy to do as the law can be counter intuitive or even stacked against landlords. You do not want to be on the wrong side of the law. Being unaware of the law will not be an excuse. Every judge you go before will expect you to know and understand your local landlord laws no matter your level of experience.

4. **Location, Location, Location** – What are the three most important words in real estate? Location, location, location! If you have never heard that saying before, please commit it to memory. You must know the local market you are investing in. What do I mean by "local?" Local is wherever you decide to invest. When thinking about a location you should think about the following questions: What are good locations? What are not-so-good locations? What are the local rental rates? What are local properties selling for? If you do not know this basic information, how will you ever know you are getting a good deal or if your cash flow will be positive? Do not rely completely on others for this information. You need to do your own due diligence. Know that not everyone out there is trustworthy. Some are going to try to take advantage of your newbie naiveté and scam you.

5. **You Will Never Stop Fixing Things** – There will be repairs, and then there will be more repairs. The repairs will never stop. You will need to put aside money each and every month to make repairs. Even if the property you bought is brand new or has just been completely rehabbed, plan on repairs. Tenants have an amazing capability to break stuff.

    The standard measure is to budget about 10 percent of your gross rents for repairs. That means if your property rents for $1,000 per month, set aside $100 for repairs. After years in the business I can say that, at least for me, this number is perhaps a bit low. I often invest in older buildings, so my costs may be a bit higher. In any event, the point is that you need to budget for repairs. They never seem to stop.

6. **Tenants Rarely Stay Put** – Most tenants will move after a couple of years. It is just the nature of the business. I mention this because you need to budget for vacancies. You cannot count on being 100 percent rented 100 percent of the time, no matter where or how nice your property is. People move. People move a lot. The average tenant in

Memphis, for example, moves once per year. We have found in our business that we have a vacancy rate of about five percent. The standard, however, is about 10 percent but it may be higher or lower in your market. Again, as with repairs, that means if your property rents for $1,000 per month then be sure to budget $100 per month for a vacancy credit. In this way, you will not be caught short when the time comes for you to pay the bills, which keep on coming even while your property is vacant.

7. **Your Money Is Made When You Buy, Not When You Sell** – This statement may seem a bit backward at first, but it is very true. You make money when you buy, not the other way around. You might collect the money when you sell, but it was your insight into finding the deal in the first place that made you the money. Keep this in mind as you go out into the market looking for properties. Look for properties for which there is potential to increase the income. Buy the property right in the first place. If you buy a bad deal, it will always be a bad deal.

8. **Real Estate Investing Is Not As Cut Throat As You Think** – Sure, there is competition but many landlords love to talk about their business and most of them enjoy helping out someone who is getting started. Helping others is one of the main reasons why I still belong to my local real estate investors association. Plus, just talking with others in the same boat as I am can be a big help. Believe me when I say that many times you will feel like it is just you against the world in this business. Once you go out on your own you will not have your co-workers around anymore to complain to and blow off steam with. Having other local landlords around and available to discuss your problems or concerns is a big help. You will likely have no problem or issue that other landlords have not dealt with before. So, get out there and talk to other landlords. Develop a contact list of people you can

call when you hit a bump. Do not be afraid or wary of talking with other landlords. Most are more than willing to share and to help you.

9. **Liars Are Everywhere** – There are so many people out there that will lie to you. They will try to sell you all kinds of sob stories or dreams to wear down your defenses. Do not fall for it and do not let them wear you down.

   Who lies?

   Applicants lie. Property sellers lie. Tenants lie. Everyone lies. Phrases like "great cash flow," "newly renovated," or "100% occupied," and "I'll pay you on Tuesday," will all sound great but could be pure BS. To see through the lies and avoid getting sucked into a bad deal, you need to understand the real estate numbers. The numbers do not lie. To understand the numbers, however, you have to learn the business and do your own research. Falling for a lie can mean falling for a very bad deal. One bad deal can have a lot of zeros on the end of it. Verify everything with your own research.

10. **Cash Flow Is King** – Cash flow is what keeps your business running, through both the good and the bad times. Everything else is a bonus that you should never, ever bet on. Keep in mind that there was a real estate crash in 2008. Real estate will not always go up in value and it can leave you hanging when you most need it. Always, always remember that cash flow is king.

Do you still want to get into real estate investing and landlording after reading all of this? I hope you do. Despite all of the issues described above, real estate investing and landlording are still some of the best ways to build wealth and change your life for the better. Plus, if these points have not scared you away, then I think that you just might succeed in this business. Being aware of the potential trials and tribulations on the front end is a big step in the right direction towards success. Keep at it. The rewards of real estate investing will outweigh the growing pains you experience.

No Money or Experience? No Problem. Here Is What You Need To Do

If you lack bundles of cash and real estate investing experience, you might think that you cannot get into real estate investing. You are wrong. You can still get into real estate and be successful, even with little money and less experience.

Don't believe me? Well, it is true and I am going to share with you how you can do it. All you need to do is go and find a good real estate deal.

Finding a good real estate deal will put you on the path towards success. There are always other investors looking for good deals that will gladly pay you for them. In fact, if the deal is good enough, you may very well have a bidding war over your deal. Do you need money to find this deal? Perhaps a little bit, but certainly not thousands. Can you make thousands from this deal? Yes. Does that solve the money problem? Yes as well.

What about your lack of experience? Don't you need the experience to find the deal? Experience helps, but it is not necessary. What is necessary is the knowledge of how to find and secure a good deal. That knowledge can be acquired. You can acquire it just as easily as the next person can.

Get started by following the steps outlined below. If you do, you will be well on your way towards real estate success without a lot of money or experience.

1. **Pick A Place To Farm** – No, I do not mean cultivating wheat. I mean cultivating real estate. You need to select an area that you think would be a good place to farm, or dig, for real estate deals. It does not have to be an entire city, county or metro area. In fact, I think it should be a more specific location so you can focus your efforts. It could be the neighborhood where you live or it could be near your place of work. Your farm could be the trendy part of town, or it could

be the working class area of town. Learn what properties in that area are selling for. Get a grasp of what property values are. Get to know this information so you can either negotiate or recognize a potential deal when it comes along.

2. **Get To Know Other Investors** – While you are farming your local market, you need to find people who are buying in that market. You need to find people that will want your deal. Find a way to meet and work with other investors. Your area will hopefully have a local Real Estate Investors Association. If not, peruse the forums of real estate websites or look for other types of business association meetings in your area. Look at who owns and who is buying properties (local newspapers will often tell you). Get out there and talk to people. Ask about the types of deals they are looking for and the areas they want to do business in. Develop a contact list that you can use in the future. Upon talking with people, you may just figure out how to tailor your efforts to fit other investor needs and thus help you be successful.

3. **Get Out There And Look Around** – This is where the rubber will meet the road and where all of that work involved in real estate investing takes place. Farming an area not only means learning about property values, it also means getting out there and physically looking for properties and making the deal happen. It is doubtful that you or your realtor, if you use one, are going to find many good deals on the MLS or on some other website. The competition there is just too intense. You need to find the deals before others do. Doing this takes work on the ground. It takes cultivation. How do you do it?

   a. **Drive for Dollars** – One of the best ways to find a deal is to do what is called "Driving for Dollars." Driving for dollars is exactly what it sounds like. You drive around and look for properties that could be deals in the area you chose to farm. What are you looking for? It could be all sorts of things, including tall grass, deferred maintenance, a general unkempt look, etc. After driving around a bit you will see what I am talking about. This technique can really work well. Make a list while you drive. Talk to neighbors if you can. Do anything legal to find out more about a property and a potential deal.

b. **Send Snail Mail** – After driving around and gathering your list, go back to your home or office and do something very simple; look up the owner and send them a letter asking to buy their property. Make it a personalized handwritten letter so it gets opened and read. Do not make it too fancy or wordy. All you need to say is "I noticed your property and I want to buy it."

c. **Rinse And Repeat** – Drive for dollars and send letters again and again. People will not always respond to your first attempt so several letters over time may be needed. If you keep at it, a deal will eventually come your way.

4. **Get The Property Under Contract** – Once a deal comes your way you need to learn how to secure it. You need to learn how to get it under contract so you can market it to other investors. Do not, I repeat, do not simply negotiate a deal and then market it to others without getting it under contract. There are dishonest people out there who will steal your deal and leave you with nothing. There are no handshake deals. Learn how to protect yourself by getting a deal under contract. A contract does not have to be complicated. Mine is generally only one page and lists the address, the price, a closing date, has a clause for adequate financing and space for signatures. Little more is needed and I go into contracts a lot more in Section 3.

5. **Market Your Deal** – Once you have your deal secured under contract, now is the time to put it out there to all of those investors you got to know. Get on the phone. Send out texts and emails.

Hopefully, your deal will be so good they will be banging on your door.

6. **Get Paid** – Real estate contracts are generally assignable. That means you can transfer your contract (assign it) to someone else for a fee. For example, say you get the owner of 123 Main Street to agree to sell you the property for $100,000. You can assign that contract to another investor for a fee, say $5,000. They then pay you $5,000 and you assign the contract to them. They close on the property paying the owner the $100,000 price you negotiated. Your efforts and hard work netted you $5,000. Treat yourself to a reward for a job well done. And guess what? Now you are an experienced investor.

That is all there is to getting started in real estate investing with little money or experience. It is not the quick and easy answer, but nothing worth doing or having is ever really quick and easy. Real estate investing takes work. If you work at it and follow these steps, you really can be successful.

What Newbies (And Seasoned Investors) Simply Must Master

When you saw the title to this chapter I bet many of you immediately began to think about some of the more concrete components of real estate investing such as contracts, spreadsheets or some sort of app. While those are important, when getting started in real estate investing there are some more intrinsic elements that you need to master to be successful that are a bit more complex than apps or contracts. Honestly, some of them are components that none of us may ever truly master. They are aspects of real estate investing that we have to keep learning about and striving to improve on every day.

What are these more intrinsic components of real estate investing?

1. **The Market** – Markets can be quite unforgiving. Markets will not care if you do not understand how they are working. Nor will they care if you do not look before you leap. This is their beauty. It is how they were designed to work. Mistakes are quickly left behind and misallocated resources are redistributed to those with better judgment. While this may not be to your liking, it has to be that way. In order to rebalance, the market has to quickly clear out those that make mistakes.

   On the other hand, mastering your market can provide you with everything you have ever dreamed of having. Mastering your market comes down to knowing and understanding where you plan to invest. Knowledge and understanding will lead to sound decisions, and sound decisions are best to avoid mistakes.

   So what market are you going to invest in? Can you define and describe it? Who is buying in that market? Who is selling in that market? Why? What are the price points? What is this market telling you about the future? Mastering the answers to these questions and more will lead you towards mastering that market. It will allow to you spot potential profit-making opportunities.

Mastering all of this will take time. Plus, you really never can stop learning about your market because markets change all of the time. Always be working to master you market. Others will be. If you can do it better, you will be very, very successful.

2. **The Analysis** – The analysis of a potential deal is one of the most important things real estate investors do. Proper analysis is a key part to being successful. Doing the analysis and running numbers will tell you when to stop, when go forward, or proceed with caution.

How much analysis is enough and how much is too much? Two very difficult questions to answer as every potential deal will be different. Newbies have to realize that you cannot get perfect numbers every time. Some are just going to have to be your best guess. You will have no way of knowing for sure what a property will sell for, how long it will take to sell or if there is a major repair lurking behind those walls. You just have to use your knowledge, along with the knowledge and experience of others, to give it your best, educated guess and move forward. As discussed previously, there will be some risk involved.

You cannot wait forever or take too long with your analysis, however. Instead, you have to be fairly quick and adept at doing it. If you wait too long, if you feel that every number simply has to be perfect before you pull the trigger, guess what will likely happen? You will never do a deal because others will grab them while you were waiting for a better analysis. At some point, if you want to be successful, you are going to have to master the art of analysis. It is definitely an art. An art that uses calculated and informed guesses to take a risk. Master the analysis, give it your best educated guess, and take the plunge.

3.   **Fear** – Fear can be a huge mountain to climb and overcome. Fear is one of our most basic emotions. We have it because it has kept us alive over the millennia. A bit of fear is actually a good thing and there are, to be honest, lots of things in real estate investing to be fearful of. Lots of dollars are at stake, for example. Plus, striking out on your own and doing something totally new, something where you are not completely sure what the result will be is a scary thing. There are people, such as property owners and contractors, who you have never dealt with before. And then there are the internal fears. What if I make a mistake? What if I fail? *What if? What if? What if?* Real estate investing is full of unknowns and we as humans do not like unknowns. They cause fear and therefore there will be fear, sometimes a lot of fear. That's okay, as long as you do not let it overpower and stop you from moving forward.

These fears are quite valid. You may even feel like you should turn around and run away sometimes. I know I did (and sometimes still do). I also know that you have to master those fears, take the step forward and try. I can also tell you that once you do take that first step, you will look back and wonder what you were ever fearful of. Nothing is better to conquer fear than experience, and there is no way to get experience other than by doing. Trust me. It will get easier and easier every time. Fear will then be someone else's problem.

4.   **Themselves** – You may not have thought of this one, but the last thing you have to master is yourself. You will be going somewhere you have never been before. It will be ever changing and constantly evolving. It will be very hard at times and you may very well feel like giving up. Your brain will want to take the easy way out. It will want you to go back to what you know. It will want you to give up your dreams in return for that comfort zone you once hated.

Do not listen to your brain this time. You will need to master your thoughts and yourself.

Mastering these items can be easier said than done. Some days will be really tough but remember, everything, no matter how bad or depressing, will pass. Remember why you wanted to get into real estate investing. Remember your dreams and stay focused on the future.

Develop goals and strive to reach them. Not lofty unattainable goals, but something realistic, like buying your first investment property next month or making your first $10,000. Change your spending habits and how you use your time. Develop a budget and turn off Netflix. It may take time, but eventually your brain will change its tune and I think that you will really like the person you become.

Some of the above may simply sound like mental exercises or like I am trying to teach a psychology course. The fact of the matter is that becoming a successful real estate investor often involves mental exercises and changing your personal psychology. You have to have the right information, attitude, and mindset to be successful. It has to be right there, at the front of your brain and ready for you to use.

What Should A Newbie Real Estate Investor Be Cautious Of?

Newbies are filled with dreams, enthusiasm and excitement. They are often chomping at the bit to get started. Newbies are also ignorant and somewhat gullible. They can be unsure of whom they should trust and blind as to whom they should not.

Being a newbie therefore puts one in a somewhat vulnerable position. I have seen vulnerable newbies get themselves into jams over the years and I still see it today. Their inexperience acts as a sort of blinder. They are not yet fully aware of the trouble they can get into and their eagerness to get started can cause them to let down their guard.

Newbies can overcome this problem by learning. Not just about investing techniques, numbers and financing, but also things to be on guard for, things that they should be cautious of. It may sound strange, but just knowing that you do not know can save you from a lot of trouble. What should a newbie learn to be cautious of? Here are some thoughts.

1. **Be Cautious Of Going In Too Fast** – Please be careful about going in too fast. Breathe. Chill. Relax. Your time for a deal will come. Remember there are and will be plenty of deals out there. You need to take time to learn about your market and how to put together a good deal. I understand your excitement, but reading one book or attending a one-day seminar is just not enough. I am not telling you that you need to spend thousands or tens of thousands on your real estate education. Nor am I telling you to never make the jump because you can never acquire all of the knowledge you need. You just need to know when the time is right for you, and when you have enough knowledge to go forward. How much is enough? Hard to say but it will feel right to you and you will know the time has come. Moving too quickly will get you in a heap of trouble and bad deals can be very hard to get out of.

2. **Be Cautious Of Taking On A Project You Are Not Prepared To Handle** – Please do not take on a burned-out shell of a building as your first rehab (unless of course you have been working as a contractor for the last 10 years, *even then* be careful). Please do not buy a 50-unit apartment building as your first investment property. While these properties can be good investments and opportunities, they are also perhaps a bit too complicated for the newbie investor. Remember you are new and learning. The big trial by fire may not be the best first step. It is perhaps better to take on a less strenuous project such as a single family house or a quad-plex in a decent neighborhood requiring minimal repairs. Doing so will get you into the game, allow you to gain valuable experience and, best yet, keep you in the game for bigger and better projects later on.

3. **Be Cautious That You Might Not Really Like Real Estate Investing** – Being a real estate investor is many things, but if you think that it is going to be a completely hands-off thing you can do from the comfort of your living room you have another thing coming. I did not write this to sell you a dream, and I want you to get into real estate with your eyes wide open. You need to know that it will require work, sometimes hard work and sometimes thankless work. The rewards can be great and real estate investing will help you fulfill your dreams. Some people thrive in real estate; others, however, decide it is not quite what they bargained for. Thing is you can't really tell until you do it. Stick your toe in first to see if the water is to your liking.

4. **Be Cautious Of Reaching Too Far** – If you have some cash, great! Just be sure to keep some of it. Your lack of experience often comes with zeros attached to it. What do I mean by that? I mean that your lack of experience will potentially cost you a lot of money. Keep some of your cash for reserves. You WILL need it. Cash will give you options when you need them most. Do not overextend and plunge in

with everything you have all at once. After all, what if you hate it? Plus, you might not be able to recover financially and mentally.

5. **Be Cautious Of Taking On Too Much** – Some people want the world and they want it now. They want to buy and hold, flip, rehab, retail, wholesale. It's easy after all, they said so on HGTV. This approach of taking on too much will often cause you to have a loss of focus. This loss of focus will often lead to burnout, which then will lead to failure. Again, why not start slow and focus your efforts on a particular investing strategy. Success is much more likely to be attained and the achievement of small goals will spur you on to bigger and better things.

5. **Be Cautious Of Trying To Massage The Numbers** – If there is one thing I have seen more newbies try and do it is attempting to make the numbers fit. They try to create a deal where one does not exist and the massaging is done because they just want that first deal to happen. Always remember that numbers do not lie and if you think you can adjust this or that number against all the advice of everyone you have talked to and all you have learned, then you will fail. Do not think that repairs and expenses will be cheaper. They will not. Do not think your vacancies will be less. They will not. The formulas behind the numbers are tried and true. Stick to them.

6. **Be Cautious Of Real Estate Gurus** – A real estate guru is someone who professionally teaches about real estate investing. There are lots of so-called gurus out there. I guess some would even call me one. That said, some want to tell how things really are and others just want to sell you a dream. Both can be enticing but you need to be aware of what you are being sold. That can be really hard. It is okay for people to talk about dreams and set goals. But, are these dreams and goals based in reality? Are they achievable? Keep in mind that real estate investing is about running a business and is it likely that you will be

heavily involved in it, at least at first. Don't fall for the hyped-up dream. Always watch out for anyone trying to sell you "multiple levels" of investing advice. If anyone wants you to "invest" more and more to get "inside" information, then be very careful. I have seen others spend thousands, even tens of thousands, on so-called education and get nowhere.

7. **Be Cautious Of Anyone Saying That You Cannot Go Wrong** – Yes, there are great deals out there. Everyone that has been in the business for a while will tell you their story of getting one. The thing that most people **will not** tell you is that good deals can be few and far between and that there are no sure things. A deal can always go wrong, especially if you are naive enough to not know what you are getting into. Be wary of anyone telling you that a deal is a sure thing and that you cannot go wrong. It is possible that it cannot, but you are inexperienced so how can you be sure? Do your homework. Run your numbers. Ask for advice. Hopefully you have found a sure thing, but I have seen more than one sure thing end up going quite wrong.

8. **Be Cautious Of Anyone Who Tempts You With Urgency** – Using urgency or the "buy now before the deal is gone" routine is one of the oldest salesman's tricks in the book. There is not a thing out there, not a property, not education, not information, that has to be purchased today. I bet if you go home and sleep on it, that offer that was pitched to you, if it is a good one, will still be there tomorrow. If it is not, then there will be others.

9. **Be Cautious Of Someone, Anyone, Saying You Have To Pay A Lot For An Education** – How many of you have an extra $10,000, $20,000 or $50,000 lying around? I know I do not and you likely do not either. That money will be much better spent on your investments and you do not need to spend it on a real estate education. You do

not need the mentoring programs that cost tens of thousands of dollars. They are just not necessary. While there may be some good information contained in them, most are just not worth it.

10. **Be Cautious Of Most Realtors** – This one may surprise you, but just because someone is a realtor does not mean that they know anything about real estate investing. Most realtors have no idea how investors work, what they do, or what a good deal is. They often have had even less education than you have. You can see this reality by examining what many realtors will claim to be a good deal. Sure, it may be a good deal to a retail buyer, but not a real estate investor. This is not to say that there are not "good" realtors out there, there are. Working with a "good" realtor can be very beneficial. However, most realtors do not know very much about real estate investing or real estate investors. That is not what they are trained to do. Do not rely on your cousin who just got their real estate license to give you real estate investing advice. Take your time and find a realtor that understands real estate investors. They are out there.

Becoming a successful real estate investor does not happen overnight. It is a process. This process does not have to cost thousands or involve overly complicated projects. How long this process takes is up to you. You should and you need to take your time and do not ever feel pressured. Be cautious of the items pointed out in this chapter. Your success will come at a pace that is right for you.

Section 3 – Buying Your First Property

It has all come down to this, your first investment property.

The first one!

 I remember buying my first investment property. I even remember taking this picture of it. In fact, I still own it. It is a duplex and I bought it to live in one side and rent out the other. I wanted to get firsthand experience and learn the ropes. I remember the excitement well. The excitement of everything you have been learning finally coming together. The excitement you feel as you begin to fulfill your dreams.

I also remember the nervousness and hesitation, especially as I was signing all of those papers at the closing table. Was I doing the right thing? Did I even know what I was doing? How could I be sure?

I sort of did. I think. Maybe. I had certainly read a lot of educational material on real estate investing and I had run the numbers to the best of my ability so I jumped in. I still had a lot to learn, though, and there was a lot I learned by just jumping right in.

At some point, you will stop the reading and jump right in, too. Let's take a look now at how to do just that.

Questions You Should Ask Yourself Before You Buy Your First Rental Property

Buying that first rental property is exciting. All of the studying you have done, all the research, the driving around, the talking to other investors, it is all finally coming together with the purchase of your first rental property. You are looking forward to building your wealth and income. You can see "Easy Street" just up ahead.

I am happy and excited you are at this point. Do you realize how many people never get this far? Lots of people read the books and blogs, buy the courses, meet with other investors, look at dozens of properties and never, ever make a move. You, however, are different and about to take that first bold step.

As I said I am happy and excited for you. But…

Before you finally pull that trigger, I want you to take a moment and think. I want you to reflect a bit. I want you to try to set all of that excitement you feel aside and take just a few moments to make sure you are really doing the right thing. You do that by asking yourself the following questions and giving yourself honest answers.

1. **Am I Sure I Understand What I Am Doing?** – I know that you have been told that real estate investing and being a landlord is a passive investment. That may be true as far as the IRS is concerned, but I am here to tell you there is nothing about landlording that is passive. Being a landlord is definitely a hands-on experience. Even if you go with a property manager or the turnkey route you still have to manage the managers and actively check on your property. There is no way around this fact.

   Being a landlord also takes tenacity and perseverance. If you are like me and you want to keep more of what you make by developing your own management techniques, then you are going to do much of this on your own. Do not underestimate it; there will be a lot to do. There will be tenants to screen, leases to write, rent to collect, repairs and maintenance, and on and on and on. Are you ready to do all of that? You will have to enforce your rules and policies and calm disputes. Are you ready to act tough? You will have to because if you let your tenants slide they will take you to the cleaners. Most of the time things work out okay and most tenants are decent people who will do the right thing. But trust me when I say that there will be times when you will wonder why you ever thought real estate was a good idea. While the rewards can be great, landlording can at times be quite the task. So make the leap, just understand what you are getting into now before you go.

2. **Am I Sure Of What The Numbers Are Telling Me?** – You simply must make sure that you understand the numbers, because if you do not you are in for a hard lesson. Remember that the numbers you are looking at are real. This is not study time anymore. This is a real-life property and there are a lot of zeros around those numbers. Are you sure you understand what the property's potential income will be? How? How did you verify it? Did you check out other nearby properties? Did you look at websites like Zillow and Rent-o-Meter? Did you talk with other landlords in your area?

Are you sure you have budgeted accurately for all expenses? Are there vacancy factors and reserves included? Please, please, please make sure that the numbers on the property you intend to buy really do work and that your cash flow is positive. Read the chapter on putting the numbers together on your first buy and hold deal and then read it again. Have you asked someone with experience, perhaps at your local real estate investors association, to look over your numbers and give advice? If not, why not?

Appreciation is generally not a good thing to bet on in the landlording business. Always remember that you are looking for cash flow. Always remember that cash flow is king. Appreciation is awesome if you can get it, but do not bet your future on it. Not yet. Get in and get some steady experience with cash flow first. Do not speculate on your first deal. Invest for the long term. Go for the cash flow.

Real estate investing is only going to give you one chance at a first impression. Please do everything you can to make it a good one so you will keep coming back. I want you to be successful on your first deal so you will buy more.

3. **Is This Deal Going To Work For Me And My Lifestyle?** – Okay so far so good. You know what you are getting into and the numbers work. Now, if like me you are going to be more hands-on at first and learn the ropes a bit, think about how this deal is going to work for you and how you plan to operate. Will you be okay traveling back and forth to this property for showings, maintenance, lockouts, etc? Is the property located in a neighborhood that you would feel comfortable in at night? How are you going to collect rent? If you need to go to the property to do so (if you need to do this think again about the property and how you plan to operate), will you feel comfortable doing so? Are you glossing over any potential issues just to get your first deal? I have seen more than one newbie landlord ignore the neighborhood characteristics, the potential tenant characteristics and even deferred maintenance because they are so keyed up on getting that first deal. Before you buy, just stop and think a bit about how this deal will affect you and your investing goals and your lifestyle. When you do, what looked good on paper may or may not seem all that great.

4. **What If I Do Not Like Real Estate?** – Most people do not even think about asking themselves this question, but it is vitally important. People get so caught up in the learning and the excitement they forget

that they might not even like real estate investing. What if you buy this property, work at it for a little while and then decide that landlording is not for you? What will you do then? Will you be able to sell the property? Maybe. Perhaps you can turn the property over to a management company, but that comes with its own set of problems and additional costs that may tip the cash flow negative. What will you do if this landlording thing does not work out? Now is a good time to ask yourself what happens if you do not like it.

5. **How Will I Get Out Of This?** – Do you want to be a landlord forever? Maybe. Maybe not. While holding on to your properties until you die is a viable strategy, I would bet many of you would like to cash out at some point and move on to greener pastures. Now is the perfect time to think about this question because as I have said elsewhere, you make your money when you buy, not when you sell.

Think about how long you intend to hold this property. Is it for five, ten, twenty years or more? When you are ready to sell who will you sell it to? The thing about investment properties is that most often there is little if any retail market for them. That being the case, as a new investor you have to understand that the only person you are likely going to sell to at some point in the future is another investor. Think about that. What will that future investor be looking for? Most likely it will be the same things you were looking for, which is a deal. If they are smart, they will be asking themselves these same questions. Landlording is generally a **long-term** investment strategy. Do not think that you are going to jump in and then be able to jump right back out. Jumping back out often comes with a very significant cost. As I said before, there are a lot of zeros attached to those numbers. It may very well cost you later if you do not think about it now. So think about your long term goals and how you plan to get out of and sell your real estate investments in the future.

Make sure that real estate investing is the right thing for you by asking yourself these five questions before you make that first purchase. The hype and excitement is easy to get caught up in and HGTV can make it look so easy. Remember that TV is not reality. Take a few minutes to sit back and think. Think about these five questions. You may very well save yourself a lot of money and frustration.

Preparing to Buy Your First Investment Property—Getting Your Own House In Order

Before you buy that first investment property, you need to get prepared. Not as far as getting into the spirit of things, as I'm sure that has already happened. You need to get prepared by defining what you want to buy, determining how much you can afford and where the money will come from.

If you're like me, you most likely do not have piles of cash sitting around looking for something to do (congrats to you if you do). You are most likely going to have some skin in the game but you are also going to have to find other people's money (OPM) to buy that first investment property.

There is plenty of OPM out there but the thing is you are going to have to get your own house in order before you can consider buying another one. Think about it. We all have friends who have massive amounts of disorder in their lives, would you lend them money? I hope not, at least not until they got their house in order.

So while you are learning about all of the wonderful benefits of real estate investing, here are seven things you need to do to get your own house in order so you can be prepared to buy that first investment property.

1. **Define Your First Investment Property Goal** – What type of property do you want to buy? Is it a house, a duplex or a multi-family property? Why? Where will it be located? Will you live in your first property like I did? If so, how long do you intend to live there? How quickly will you be looking to sell—five, ten, fifteen years? Answering these and other questions related to your investing goals will narrow down and refine your search. They will also provide you with the focus needed to find your first deal.

2. **Determine Your Price Range** – How much can you afford to put into real estate investing? Is it $50,000, $100,000 or $1,000,000? What will your initial investment budget be? Whatever it turns out to be, going straight to the top of your limit is perhaps not the best idea when starting out. You do not want to purchase anything that could bust your budget. Focus on properties that are a bit below the top of your price range when starting out. Why? Your inexperience can cause too many things to go wrong and you do not want your entire financial life on the line over your first property. How do you determine your price range? You do it by examining where you are financially, what you can borrow, what you can use as a down payment and the market you wish to invest in.

3. **Get Smart** – Learn about your loan options and what their consequences are. What does it take to get OPM? You should be able to have intelligent conversations with various lenders about your options. Always keep your options open and do not let anyone push you towards any particular product. This is your purchase and you are in control. If someone does not seem to want to discuss different options, then find other people to talk to. Other people's money can take many forms and you need to choose the one that will work best for you.

4. **Get Your Financial Life In Order** – Now is the time to create a written household budget if you do not have one. Figure out how to live below your means and cut unnecessary expenses. Save! Put money away each month. Pull your credit report and review it. Make sure that everything is correct on the report. One in four people have a mistake on their credit report and these mistakes can prevent you from getting OPM when a deal comes along. It is best to get ahead of that issue now before you miss out. Also make sure your income taxes are complete and in order. Pull all of this material together and put it in one folder for easy and quick access. Almost any lender you go to is

going to want all of that information and if you can pull it together quickly and in an organized fashion you will leave a good impression. That impression can be very important.

5. **Save Money, But Also Keep Track Of The Sources** – Save your money. It will provide you with options later on when you need one most. Lenders these days also like to see some reserves and you may likely need a down payment of some type. Thing is, you will need to demonstrate where the money came from. Lenders will not trust how the money got into your account or where you got it. Thus, you will need to verify the sources of your money for them. Several months of a budget, a savings plan and bank statements will do just that. Seems strange, but you need to be able to show that you are not borrowing from someone else to fund your reserves or down payment. Lenders are simply trying to lessen their risk with a first time real estate investor. Best to prepare for that now and by doing so you will again make a good first impression.

6. **Find Knowledgeable People To Work With** – There are some truly knowledgeable real estate people out there who will be happy to work with and help you. Who are these people? These people are Realtors, other investors, bankers, CPAs, etc. They can advise you on your real estate journey and help you make the right decisions. Where can you find these people? Referrals are the best way and once you find one solid, knowledgeable person to work with, they will refer others to you. You can start with the real estate agent that sold your aunt's house if you want to, but try and dig a little deeper. Look for agents that are selling to other investors. Seek out other investment property owners and ask them. You can often find many of the folks you are looking for at your local Real Estate Investors Association meetings. It is where I find many of the people I work with.

7. **Have Fun!** – Remember the first chapter? Real Estate investing is fun. Hopefully it will be for you as well. Searching for properties and going through them is just enjoyable to me. Do not let the research or the pressure stress you out too much and do not get emotionally attached to any property. The best real estate purchases are made not only when you have a clear mind, but also when you are having fun.

Motivation Is The Key

Buying properties for investment purposes is very different from buying a property to live in. As an investor you are looking at the bottom line and scrutinizing the numbers. A home buyer is looking at other important factors, such as location, schools, layout, etc. While all of these things have value, we investors are looking for a deal, and the key to getting a real estate deal is often motivation.

I am sure that you are motivated to get started, but that is not where I am going here. I am not talking about motivation on your part, but motivation on the seller's part. The seller has to be motivated to sell or there is likely no deal to be had. And the more motivation there is, the better it can be for you.

What would cause a seller to be motivated? There are numerous causes. They could have had a job transfer, a death in the family or a divorce. Evictions can create motivation and banks are generally not interested in keeping the properties they have to foreclose on. If you can find one of these, then you have the makings of a potential deal with a motivated seller.

Over the years I have found three types of sellers offer the most motivation. These are banks, tired landlords, and those that have inherited property. Gauging the level of motivation with these and other types of sellers can range from easy to difficult. Honestly, you may never know quite how motivated they are.

Banks are almost always motivated. Banks are not in the real estate investing or landlording business and do not want to be. But they are generally not stupid and will seek competent advice on what they own. They may have unrealistic prices in their heads, but they are generally motivated to sell. Most bank-owned properties will be listed with a Realtor and what I have found is that to make a deal here, banks often need to be educated on the true value of the asset they are holding. Banks are often hopeful they can recoup what they have loaned on a property. Sure, the asset may be worth the price they are asking if it was fully rented, generating top of the market rents and lacking repairs of any sort. But that is rarely the case with bank-owned properties. Thus, it often takes a little bit of time to educate the banks and work these deals.

Tired landlords are another potentially motivated seller and they are also generally going to list their properties with a Realtor as well. Many times the Realtor will list the property with what they call an "exceptional" or high price. This high price will not give you any clue as to the seller's motivation. In these circumstances, you have no idea why the owner is selling the property or how motivated they are. The owner may be retiring, he may be sick of dealing with tenants, he may have an illness, or he may not be motivated at all and only trying to gauge the market. He may just be trying to see if there is someone out there who will "pay his price" so to speak. In these circumstances when you see a property come on the market that is listed by a Realtor, you need to look for other clues to motivation. These clues could be evictions, the physical condition of the property, or even length of ownership.

You can ask the Realtor why the owner is selling, but most likely you will just receive a vague answer. If you want the property, all you can do is view it, run your numbers and make your offer based on those numbers. If the seller comes back with a counteroffer, you can begin to gauge the motivation. If no counteroffer materializes, move on—the seller is not motivated.

People who have inherited properties are also often highly motivated. Sure, they might be grateful for being left such an asset, but it is not cash. The property will not pay for the new car, boat or vacation until it sells. Heirs also now possess something that they have to maintain and spend money on. These can be very motivating factors. Sometimes heirs will list these properties with a Realtor, but sometimes they will be greedy and not want to pay a commission. They may be somewhere in between. If you can find these motivated sellers before a Realtor gets involved, you can have the makings of a very good deal.

I do not mind working with any type of seller, but most often for a property to be a good deal for me, the owners have to be motivated to sell. If the motivation is not there, the gap between what they ask and what you bid is often just too wide to bridge. It is smart for investors to try and determine the level of motivation as best they can early on. If one finds it lacking, it is often best not to waste much time and move on to the next potential deal.

It Is Best To Deal With The Property Owner "If" You Can

One of my all time frequently asked questions is "How do you find the properties you buy?"

There really is no set or standard answer to that question as I find the properties I buy in all sorts of ways. Over the years, I have found properties by responding to ads in the newspaper (is that even possible anymore?), from the Realtor's Multiple Listing System, from wholesalers, by driving for dollars, by sending letters, from bird dogs, from referrals. Like I said, I find properties all sorts of ways.

No matter how I may find the properties, being able to put together a deal that works for me is another matter. The best deals I have made generally have come about when I am able to get in touch with one specific person, the property owner.

You newbies might not have expected that answer. Newbie thinking is often more along the lines that you will work with Realtors, or other go-betweens, when negotiating a real estate deal. You should put that thinking aside because if an investor can get in touch with the owner of a property, and if the owner is somewhat motivated to sell, the investor can likely work out a pretty good deal.

The best way to buy properties and get deals therefore is by talking directly to the owner.

Why? What makes dealing directly with the property owner so much more conducive to getting good deals?

For one thing it is just you and the owner and directness equals ease. There is no Realtor involved who may be building false expectations or telling the seller that you are one of "those investors." You can talk with the seller and build rapport. You can each discuss what you want out of the deal and can tell your own side of the story. You can both negotiate. Direct contact simply lets you have more input into and the ability to affect the negotiation process.

Another great reason is that there are often no other investors involved. It is just you and the owner. There is no one else knocking on the door offering too much or promising things they can't (or do not intend) to deliver on.

These are real advantages that come from talking directly with the property owner.

However, there are two big "ifs" in this discussion. Did you notice? These "ifs" complicate what at first seems very easy. What are they?

First, I might be able to make a deal "**If** I can get in touch with the owner." This is not always as clear as it seems. The owner may not be that easy to find or may not want to be found. I therefore have to try all sorts of ways to get in touch. I write letters. I talk to landscaping crews at the property. I knock on neighbor's doors. I will go through friends of friends, if possible. Perhaps the letter carrier knows something. Be aware that not all owners will want to talk to you. Do not let it get to you if you never receive an answer or get rebuffed.

Even when you can get by the first "if" and talk to the property owner, I think the second one, "**If** they are somewhat motivated" is even more important. The property owner has to be somewhat motivated to sell. Not necessarily "fire sale and have to sell tomorrow" motivated, but just somewhat motivated. If they are not, they are just kicking tires and there is likely no deal to be made. Be ready to experience this lack of motivation scenario more often than not. "Sure I'll sell, make me an offer," is the line you will hear. Well, make an offer, but if you find motivation lacking you will not like the response. Do not spend much more time on this property. Your time will just be wasted. You need to move on.

But if there is a bit of motivation, perhaps then a deal can be worked out. Sometimes it takes a bit of effort on your part. You may need to educate the seller about what you do and what services (speed and reliability) you are bringing to the table. You may need to educate the seller on the value of their property. You may need to let them think about things a bit. You may need to let the seller's emotions subside before you can move forward. There are all sorts of scenarios you may run across and every situation is different. At least when you are dealing one-on-one with the property owner you know what the situation is and where you stand. You are somewhat in control.

Cast a wide net to find properties to buy. Look at the MLS, keep on driving for dollars and keep in touch with wholesalers. All of those techniques and more will bring potential deals your way. Also be thinking of and developing techniques to get yourself talking directly to the owner of the properties you are interested in. When you are dealing with the property owner that is often the time when the best deals can be made.

Putting The Numbers Together On Your First Buy And Hold Deal

Buy and hold properties are my bread and butter. They can be for you as well. As you have learned, buy and hold properties provide you with monthly income and generate long-term wealth. If done properly, investing in buy and hold properties will be one of the best decisions you have ever made.

The key thing to always remember about buy and hold properties is that positive cash flow is the name of the game. Buy and hold property simply **must** generate positive cash flow. Without positive cash flow, you will have monthly drafts *from* your checking account to cover expenses instead of money coming into your account and adding to your income. You want to collect checks, not write them!

Any other financial benefits such as appreciation should be considered gravy. Appreciation is a great financial benefit, but it is almost completely out of your control. Markets can and do change very rapidly sometimes. If you are betting on price appreciation you are a speculator and not an investor. There is nothing wrong with speculating, but when looking at buy and hold properties positive cash flow is the key.

Always, always, always seek out positive cash flow.

With that out of the way, the question then becomes how do you best determine if a property will generate positive cash flow? It is actually pretty simple to do. First, you need to determine how much income a property will generate. Most of the time income will equal rent, but there are other sources of income such as utility and vending income. For now, let's keep it simple and stick with rent.

How do you determine the rental income on a property? Source it out. Call other landlords in the area. Check websites such as Zillow or Rent-o-Meter. Scan ads on Craigslist or Backpage. Look at the websites of property managers in your area. Try to find listings that are comparable to yours and have pictures to show you the property's condition. Check as many sources as you can.

Once you have determined potential income, the next step is figure up your expenses. Expenses are more varied and, thus, require more explanation. I have put together a list of the most common expenses that you need to know about and figure into your cash flow analysis.

Principal And Interest Payments – Most of us need to borrow other people's money to acquire the buy and hold property. Your first expense is the principal and interest payment for that borrowed money. This is the one major expense that we investors have some control over on the front end. How, you ask? The control comes in the form of the price we pay for the property. Too high a price will skew the principal and interest costs up, turning a potential deal into a no-go. Remember you make money in real estate when you buy. So buy them right on the front end.

Property Taxes – The second expense is property taxes. Be sure you include every jurisdiction that can add a little piece to your property tax bill, as they vary from location to location. For example, where I currently live I only pay city and county property taxes. When I lived in Florida, I can recall that there were no less than six or seven different taxing authorities. Your local property tax assessor should be able to guide you to all of the taxing authorities. Make sure you are aware of them all. Also remember that investment properties can be taxed at different rates. Single family homes here in Tennessee are taxed at a lower rate than duplexes, four-plexes and apartments are. Check out if the property you are interested in is taxed at a higher rate. The taxing authorities will not forgive you if you make a mistake. Taxes will be due no matter what you thought had to be paid.

Insurance – Property insurance is third on the list. The cost of this expense will vary depending on your location and type of property. These first three expenses on this list make up the "major" buy and hold expenses and are sometimes collectively referred to as PITI (Principal, Interest, Taxes and Insurance). You will likely hear the term PITI thrown around a bit as you go forward in your real estate investing career. Commit it to memory.

Repairs And Maintenance – Properties always have something that needs to be fixed. Plus there is never ending routine maintenance such as keeping the yard cut, raking leaves, cleaning gutters, painting, etc. Budget approximately 10 percent of your gross rents in this category. In other words, if monthly rental income is $1,000, budget about $100 per month for repairs and maintenance. The bill will not always be exactly $100 per month. Some months will be higher and some will be lower but over the course of time 10 percent is surprisingly accurate. If your property is older, I might go a little higher with this number, say perhaps 12 percent.

Vacancy – Vacancy is another expense you will have. Properties will never be 100 percent occupied 100 percent of the time. If it is not occupied, it is not generating any income, yet the bills will keep coming in and need to be paid. A good rule of thumb therefore is to budget about 10 percent of your gross rental income towards a vacancy expense. Depending on your location and market, this number can be higher or lower.

Utilities – Utilities also must be figured into the deal. There may be house electric meters or it may be common for the landlord to pay for water in your market. Market conditions will vary, as will rates. Some properties, for example, will be charged residential (lower) rates while others will be charged commercial (higher) rates. Make sure you know your market and your rates. Sometimes utility companies will help you with estimates but do not count on it. Get utility statements from the current owner before you purchase to verify utility expenses. You can ask for these, along with income and expense reports, in your offer to purchase the property.

Reserves – Reserves are something that more and more lenders are asking about these days before they make any loans. Reserves are funds that you set aside for those big future expenses such as a roof replacement. These expenses will always come if you hold a property long enough. A lot of lenders got burned in the last real estate bust because landlords did not budget for reserves (among other things) and left the bank holding a ruined property. If you are going to borrow bank funds, show them that you are going to set aside 10 percent of gross rents for major future repairs. Plus it is nice to have that money there when something major does happen. And something major *will* always happen.

Other Expenses – Other expenses could include trash removal, homeowner association fees, advertising, professional fees (for lawyers and accountants), license fees and other various taxes. These types of expenses will all vary depending on your local laws and market conditions. Sometimes I just throw in a miscellaneous category of about 2.5 percent gross rents just to be safe. Another expense would be property management fees, but I am assuming that you are like me and plan to manage your own properties. Therefore I do not include these fees in this discussion.

Once you have determined your potential income and expenses for a buy and hold deal, you then list them to determine the potential cash flow. I like to use a computer spreadsheet but good old pencil and paper works just as well. There are even apps you can get today that will calculate it all for you. Whatever you use, just make sure you do it.

An example will help pull all of this together. Let's say I am looking at a single family house that will rent for $1,000 per month. The owner is asking $50,000. Is that a deal that will work for you?

Assume, for this example, that I will borrow the entire purchase price of $50,000 at seven percent interest with a 20-year amortization. Those terms make my principal and interest payment $387.65 per month. There are loan calculators all over the internet that can help you figure out your principal and interest payments for borrowing other people's money. Simply do a search for "loan calculator."

Finally, let's also assume that there are no major renovations needed for this property. It is ready to go, as is.

Here is a list of all of the potential income and expenses.

Income (monthly)	**$1,000**
Expenses (monthly)	
Principal and Interest	$387.65
Taxes	$50
Insurance	$30
Repairs/Maintenance (10% of gross rents)	$100
Vacancy Credit (10% of gross rents)	$100
Utilities	$0
Reserves (10% of gross rents)	$100
Misc.	$25
Total Expenses (monthly)	$792.65
Cash Flow – Income less Expenses (monthly)	**$207.25**

$207 is pretty good monthly cash flow. Is it a deal that works for you? That will of course depend on your goals but this one seems like a no brainer to me. **It is a buy.**

Now imagine buying ten of these buy and hold properties. They would generate about $24,000 per year in positive cash flow! What could you do with that extra money? This positive cash flow is why buy and hold deals are my bread and butter. Always, always remember positive cash flow is king.

Buyer Beware

As I have noted throughout this book, cash flow is king in the landlording business. Knowing that, many property sellers will hype up their properties as excellent producers of cash flow. These sellers, at a minimum, want to attract your interest and at worst want to get one over on you. Thus, as with everything else in life, you as a buyer, especially a newbie buyer, must beware of the hype. No one is going to stop you from walking into bad deal if you do not know what you are doing. In fact, some may lead you right into it if you are not careful. You have to be educated and aware enough to see through them and their hype.

Investment properties are often advertised as excellent cash flow generators. These ads can be found everywhere, including the Realtor's listing system, on other websites, in emails and in text messages. Here is an example of what might be advertised:

2020 Anywhere Street—Awesome Cash Flow!

Rental Income	$1,500
Principal and Interest	$550
Insurance	$250
Taxes	$250
Total Cash Flow	**$500 Per Month!**

And at first glance, this property does appear to be an awesome deal with $500 of positive cash flow per month. Those of us with a bit more knowledge and experience know that there are a few pieces to the above property puzzle that are missing. Were these pieces left out through ignorance or on purpose? Who knows and it does not matter. What matters is that the potential buyer (you) is aware that they are missing. Hopefully, you already know what is missing, but if you do not, or need a refresher, here is what those pieces are.

Vacancy – No property is going to stay rented 100 percent of the time. Vacancies do not generate any income. Plus there will be costs associated with moving tenants in and out. You need to budget for at least 10 percent of your gross rents towards a vacancy factor. Thus, in the above example, if rental income is $1,500 per month, another $150 should be added to the expense side of the equation.

Repairs And Maintenance – Things break and they are going to have to be fixed. If they are not, you can expect larger vacancies or even legal hassles. You should expect to pay about 10 percent of your gross rents in repair expenses. So again, as in the example above, add another $150 to the expense side of the equation. Do you actually spend $150 every month? No. But over the course of time, it is amazing how repairs end up totaling about 10 percent of gross rents.

Reserves – Nothing lasts forever. Roofs, air conditioners and water heaters will all need to be replaced at some point. When these things break down, you are going to have to come up with the funds to replace them. These can be big ticket items and you cannot rely on insurance as they are not in the business to pay claims for normal wear and tear. Again, you should be putting aside about 10 percent of gross rents for future reserves. Add another $150 to the expense side of the equation.

Property Management – If you are going to manage the property yourself you can skip this part. You will be screening the tenants, doing the showings and fielding the complaints. If not, you are likely going to hire a management company or perhaps buy a property from a turnkey operation that already has management in place. Either way, they are also going to take a cut of the cash flow. On average this cut is about 10 percent of gross rent and adds another $150 to the expense side of the equation.

Now that we have all parts of the puzzle, let's look at that monthly cash flow for our example at 2020 Anywhere Street again.

2020 Anywhere Street

Rental Income (Monthly)	$1,500
Principal and Interest	$550
Insurance	$250
Taxes	$200
Vacancy Factor	$150
Repair Expense	$150
Capital Reserves	$150
Property Management	$150
Total Expenses (Monthly)	$1,600
Total Cash Flow (Monthly)	-$100

Quite a difference when you plug in **all** of the expected expenses. The property actually has a **negative $100** cash flow. If you buy this property, you will be writing checks every month instead of collecting them.

Beware that sellers are going to hype up their properties. They are trying to create buzz to sell their properties. This buzz may be innocent or it may be purposeful. Sometimes sellers may not know all that is involved in running a rental property business and other times they will be trying to deceive you. It is up to us, the buyers, to know and understand what we are doing and how to calculate actual cash flow. No law will be able to protect you. Buyer beware!

Making Your Offer

You have found a motivated property owner, run your numbers and everything is coming together. The positive cash flow is there and you are ready to make an offer. Take a moment and congratulate yourself, as most will never get this far. Then, take another moment and breathe.

If you are like me, the first time I was ready to make an offer I was so nervous that I could not stop pacing around. The butterflies in my stomach had swarmed harder than I could ever remember. I was nervous because I was going into uncharted territory. I had never been in this position before and it is likely you have not either. I know how you feel, but try to relax. Making an offer on a property is a good thing, it is what you have worked and studied for. Look forward to it.

When making your offer, my advice is to keep things simple.

If possible, verbally discuss your position with the property owner. I know this can be difficult for you when first starting out (trust me, it gets easier), but the best way I have found to make an offer is to just come out and say it. Tell the property owner what your numbers are telling you. Yes, leave a little wiggle room for negotiation, but just be honest and let the property owner know your position.

There are people out there who advise to never be the first to say a number. To let the property owner tell you what they will sell the property for. That can be nice if you can get the owner to do it, but I am here to tell you that many will not. They want to her what you have to offer. Do not wait or try too hard to get a number out of them. That is just going to make them mad and potentially cost you a deal. Instead, be forthcoming about what you can do and what you can offer.

If the owner does not like your offer, it is no big deal. They will just say no. And honestly, you are going to hear the word "no" a lot more than you will hear "yes." If you get a "no" answer, do not worry too much about it. You did nothing wrong. Either continue negotiating or move on and find the next potential deal.

Sometimes, after a little bit of back and forth negotiation you will get to yes. Again, try to keep things simple.

If you get a verbal yes, you now need something much more legally binding. You need to write up a contract, collect signatures and exchange some earnest money. As an investor, you should have a contract for the purchase and sale of real estate with you and ready to go. You never know when someone will say yes, and when they do you need to be able to strike when the iron is hot so to speak and have a purchase and sale contract at the ready.

The purchase and sale contract that I use is at most two pages long. Like I said, try to keep things simple. I do not want my sellers to have to read 15 pages of legalese. I want them to keep saying yes, and a lot of legalese confuses the matter and confusion is often a sure path towards no.

What should be in your contract? Some of that will depend on local customs and laws, and contract customs and laws can vary widely across the country and across the world. In general however, there are 10 items that should be in every purchase contract.

1. **The names of the property owner and the buyer.**

2. **The address (and/or legal description) of the property being purchased.**

3. **The purchase price.**

4. **The amount of earnest money.**

5. **Where the earnest money will be held and by whom.**

6. The date the contract should be completed or close.

7. A clause regarding clear and marketable title.

8. A financing clause.

9. A space for any other terms and conditions

10. A place for buyer and seller to sign and date.

That is it. There really is no need for much more. However, I should explain what a few of those items are and why you need them.

Items 1, 2, and 3 are pretty straightforward. Let me explain 4 and 5 a bit further.

Real estate purchase and sale contracts (and many other contracts for that matter) need what is legally called "consideration." There has to be some consideration given from the buyer to the seller for the contract to be valid. Consideration in this case is money, or an earnest money deposit. This deposit can be for any amount you negotiate but for single family residential real estate it is common to have an earnest money deposit of at least $1,000. You can always offer more and in some situations it may be wise to do so as it may sweeten your offer.

This deposit is held in escrow or kept by someone, often a third party and usually an attorney or title agency, and is credited back to the buyer when the sale of the property is completed. This deposit is a sort of guarantee that you, the buyer, will do what you say you are going to do and follow the terms of the contract and buy the property. Be warned, if you decide to back out simply because you got cold feet, you can forfeit your deposit to the seller. This is why a seller will generally want to negotiate for a larger deposit. Offering a large deposit is one way that you can strengthen your offer as it shows you intend to close the deal.

Item 6 is also pretty clear. There is no standard as to when a real estate deal should be completed. It can be in 24 hours or in a year. It will only depend on what you and the seller decide upon. Most contracts allow for about 30 days for the sale to complete, but be creative here if you need to be. If the seller wants to stay through Thanksgiving, which is two months away, let them. Be flexible and get the deal.

The title described in item 7 is what actually will transfer to you with the sale of the property. It is nothing more than a piece of paper that is recorded in public records that says you own the property. You want that title to be **"clear and marketable"** meaning that the property is free from liens (others claiming a right to the property) and that you can sell it. A title search will determine if the title is "clear and marketable." A good bit of advice at this point is to always buy title insurance to insure that you will always have clear and marketable title. It is pretty cheap and you just never know. Mistakes are made. Title insurance is purchased from specialized title insurance companies. You can find them in any location with a quick Google search or just ask your attorney or other real estate investors.

The next item is very important. Always put a clause in your contract that states the contract is contingent upon you receiving adequate financing. What is adequate financing? Whatever you decide it is. It could be a bank, it could be a private lender, and it could be your own money. Why is this clause so important? For one thing, you are likely not using your own money to purchase the property, so you need this clause in case your financing suddenly dries up, which it can.

Generally, this clause also gives you an out if you need it. If you discover something later on that makes this good deal bad, or something happens in your life, you can decide whatever financing you have is not "adequate" and void the contract. I do not suggest ever doing this unless **ABSOLUTELY NECESSARY** because you should be a person of your word. Do not make a deal unless you fully intend to follow through. I have never used

113

this clause and never intend to. I do not make deals that I do not intend to complete and neither should you. But, life is crazy and you just never know, so it is best to have some way out if you need it.

Finally, have a section for other clauses. What other clauses might you need? You could add a clause that you are purchasing the property in "as is" condition, or state that you will have the property inspected at a later date. You might need clauses concerning tenants if there are any in the property. Or there could be a thousand other things. I have written in clauses that the seller gets to keep a particular light fixture. Sometimes that is what it takes to get the deal done. It is up to you and what you can negotiate. But remember, try to keep it simple.

Now that you have made an offer and signed a contract, all you need to do is go to "closing" and complete the sale. What happens there? Read the next chapter to find out.

My Offer Was Accepted! Now What?

Congratulations! You negotiated an offer and it was accepted. You have a signed contract and earnest money has been exchanged. You almost have your first property under your belt. Now what? Just sit back and wait? No. You have to work at getting your contract completed or closed. You have to work at doing what you said you were going to do, be it inspecting the property, getting the money together or just showing up to sign the papers. This work can be a little or a lot depending on what it is that you negotiated. You often have very little time to do these things so you have to get moving immediately or your deal may be lost.

In this chapter, I want to go over the most common and important contract clauses that you will likely have to fulfill in order for you to make sure that you get your first deal closed.

Get The Money Rolling – Most likely you will not be using your own funds to purchase the property. You are hopefully using other people's money to finance your purchase. If you are, you need to get that money lined up and ready to go. Most lending institutions will not simply write you a check because you asked. There are procedures and paperwork. Whoever your lender is, get them on the phone and let them know about your deal. They need to get the ball rolling on their end.

Get A Title Search – After the money, the next most important thing you need done is a title search on the property you are purchasing. You want to be sure that you are purchasing a property with a **clear** title. In other words, you want to be sure that you will be able to actually own the property. A good title search will try to ensure that the person you are buying it from actually and properly owns it. A title search will try to ensure that there are no heirs or liens out there that could "cloud" your title. No title search is perfect, so I recommend that you always purchase title insurance on any property you buy. It is cheap and if you ever need it, you will be glad you have it.

Conduct Inspections – I never purchase a property without inspecting it, all of it. I will take a look in every room, in the attic, at the roof and underneath if I can. If I feel some issue is beyond my expertise and knowledge, I bring in a trusted contractor to help me evaluate the property. As someone who is just starting out, you may want to hire a property inspector to inspect the property. It is best to know exactly what you are getting into before you close and complete your purchase.

Draw Up The Paperwork – Someone will need to draw up property deeds. These deeds are done according to local laws and customs and are then recorded at the local Register of Deeds office. You can do this yourself, but that is not recommended or even allowed if you are borrowing money from a bank. You should use a good real estate attorney to draw up these documents for you. Often, the people conducting the title search described above can draw up these documents for you. They will make sure everything is legal and they will be able to finalize things with your seller. You can often find a good title company at your local real estate investors association.

Other Items – There could potentially be a whole host of other items that you have to take care of to make sure you fulfill the terms of your contract. You could have to collect leases from existing tenants. You might need a property line survey or other type of report. Whatever you negotiated in your contract, now is the time to make sure it gets done and gets done right.

Go To Closing! – That is it. You are finished. Now all you need to do is go to your attorney's office and sign your name a few times. Once you do, you will be the proud owner of your first investment property. Congratulations. That was not too hard was it? Now, go do it again.

Section 4 – Introductory Real Estate Investing Business Tips

By this point in the book you have realized that real estate investing is a business. To be successful, you have to run your investments like a business. You have to think like a CEO and work on your business, expanding it and making it leaner, meaner and better than your competition.

Looking back, this is one area I wish I had been better informed on. When I started out, I was too worried about working *in* rather than working *on* my business. I was more focused on doing repairs and cutting grass.

You need to be a person that works *on* their business rather than in it. It is very tempting to believe that you can do all of the things that need to be done at your properties better and cheaper than anyone else. I am here to tell you that thinking like that will only slow you down and ultimately hurt you if you do not change it.

It took me a little while to learn the lesson so I put the following chapters together in hopes that I can spare you from learning this lesson the hard way. Getting out of the nine-to-five world and into full-time real estate investing can and will be very exciting. It can also be overwhelming and it is easy to get lost in the many aspects of the business. You have to be always focused on how to grow your business. To do that you cannot be mired down in the details of it.

Putting The Pieces Together —What It Takes To Be A Successful Landlord

Owning a few investment properties does not automatically equal success. Acquiring investment properties is only one piece of the real estate success puzzle. There are a lot more pieces that must be put together for complete success. These pieces have to be acquired through learning and experience. It is through learning and experience that true success in the real estate investment world is found. Money will only take you so far and the ignorant and inexperienced tend to lose it very quickly.

Many of these pieces tend to be buried deep within us. They will appear as you go through your real estate investing journey and gain new experience. Others will have to be learned and developed. Either way, becoming a successful landlord does not often come easy. Success will require effort on your part.

At this point in your real estate investing journey, you likely do not even realize what all of the puzzle pieces are yet. In fact, as you read through this chapter you may even be surprised at some of them. Surprised or not, the pieces I list below are what it takes to be successful. You must work towards developing and putting them together.

It Takes Being A Detective – Successful landlords have learned to investigate what they are getting into, be it properties, business partners or tenants. Successful landlords are adept at finding quality properties. They also investigate who can be trusted and they screen out who cannot. To do this successful landlords become detectives. They have to do this because buying a non-cash flowing property, getting into a ruinous partnership or letting a bad tenant get into one of their properties will unleash a torrent of problems and possibly bankrupt them.

Successful landlords develop a sixth sense for nonsense and falsehoods. They see through the lies and the hype. They become acutely aware of a person's neatness, promptness, accuracy, truthfulness and politeness and use this sixth sense to their advantage. Successful landlords learn to read the red flags of the people they meet and work with. Developing this sixth sense and becoming a detective can be difficult and take time, but it is a puzzle piece that can and must be acquired.

It Takes Sorting Out Problems – Becoming a landlord and real estate investor means facing problems you have never faced before. These problems can range from mundane to gargantuan. Most of these problems will stem from the human factor that comes with the business. Tenants, business partners, neighbors and other property owners are all human and bring the human element with them. The loss of a job, a divorce, drug use and even roommate disputes are just some of the types of problems that you may face as you move forward in your career. You are dealing with properties and people—these problems will be unavoidable. You will have to deal with them and sort them out. You will not necessarily have to solve them all, but you will need to face and quell them if you want your business to be a success.

It Takes Not Being Penny Wise And Pound Foolish – Properties need maintenance. Things will wear out and you will have to spend money. You will not like it, but it will have to be done. The more things remain in disrepair, the more it is going to cost to fix later on. That is why successful landlords are not penny wise and pound foolish. They know that they have to spend money on the front end to avoid spending (or losing) more on the back end. Good tenants and good properties are hard enough to find. Do not be a fool and lose them by not doing repairs and maintenance. Putting off repairs can lead to a downward spiral that can be very difficult to pull out of.

It Takes Being Persistent And Tough – Life happens and it will happen to you in your landlording business. Things could be humming along very well and then out of the blue there is a shock to the system. There could be a fire or a tree could fall during a storm. A tenant can fall off the wagon; lose their job and thus their ability to pay rent. Appliances get stolen or money is embezzled. Death and illness can strike without warning. Despite all of the systems and protections you put in place these things can and will still happen. Landlords have to be tough, *persistently tough*. If they are not, their business and everything they have worked for can slip away. When bad things happen, they have to be faced and learned from.

It Takes Learning How To Say No – The time will also come when a landlord not only has to be tough, but must also stand up for themselves and their business by saying no. Saying no might mean kicking a troublesome tenant out. It might mean firing a contractor. It may also mean banding together with other landlords to fight city hall. Sometimes enough is enough and successful landlords have learned to say so. Find your voice. Learn how and when to say no.

It Takes Being Reliable – Successful landlords are reliable and more importantly, are perceived as being reliable. In business, reputation can be everything. Potential tenants will review your reputation on the internet and determine if they should rent from you. Contractors all know each other and talk amongst themselves about who pays well and who is a jerk. Do not let your good name become mud. Keep your word and be someone everyone else can rely upon.

It Takes Projecting Confidence – To be successful you have to be confident in yourself and your ability to get the job done. If you do not have that confidence, you at least have to project, or fake it until you make it. How do you do that? You do it with education first and experience later. Join your local real estate investors association, talk to other investors, learn your market, tour properties and make offers. Those educational experiences will build your confidence. You will have success even after a mistake or two. And nothing breeds confidence like a little bit of success.

It Takes Being Creative — The most successful business owners are creative. They find ways to get things done, even when everyone is throwing up roadblocks. They find deals in tight markets. They make renovations come in on time and close to budget. They find and keep good tenants. All while their competition is trying to do the same thing. They say necessity is the mother of invention and I believe it to be true. The necessity to be successful will force you to be creative.

Do you think you can do and be all of that? I did not think I could when I started out. However, it came to me eventually. I had to work hard at a lot of it. Some of it came naturally, other parts did not. Some things will be hard for you, too, and some parts will already be there. Everything that I have described in this chapter can be learned. Do not be too upset if the parts described in this chapter do not yet fit you. You likely have a lot more inside of you than you think; you may be surprised at yourself. It will come to you when you need it to.

Going From A Full-time Job To Full-Time Investor

I made the jump to full-time investor over a decade ago. It was one of the most exciting and scariest things I have ever done. It was, however, a goal that I had worked towards for years. Once I caught the real estate investing bug, I could not wait to get into it. I could not wait to get more control over my life and time. That was the exciting part. The scary part was that little voice inside of my head that was always in the background asking if I was making the right move. You know the voice. It is the one that keeps you up at night and makes you wonder if you truly know what you are doing by leaving the steady income, the health insurance, and the security that comes with these things.

I can now look back and say that I truly made the right decision. Still, I can remember actually shaking a bit when I handed my boss my resignation letter. It is an enormous decision. Quitting a full-time job requires a lot of forethought and planning. It is not a decision that should be taken lightly or done overnight.

I know that some of you out there are perhaps thinking of taking that same plunge now or are working towards it. You are wondering exactly what it will take, or do not know how to begin to quit. If this describes you then this chapter is written for you. In it, I lay out some of the steps you should follow to quit your nine-to-five job and get into real estate investing full-time. Following these steps should make the task a lot easier to handle and perhaps quiet that little voice.

The first thing to do is to realize that quitting your nine-to-five job means giving up your regular and steady income. Quitting your job means going somewhere that is less predictable. In order to make the transition to full-time investor you **must** know how much money is coming in and where it is going. Thus, you need to sit down and calculate a monthly budget. To calculate your budget you will need to collect several months of income and

124

spending data since every month can be a bit different. With several months of data, you can average things out and determine approximately what is coming in and what it is costing you to live. If you have never done this you may be in for a rude awakening. You may find that things are actually pretty tight. Hopefully, you are living below your means but if you are not, you need to start doing so. Now.

After you have developed your budget and figured out what is coming in and where it is going the second step is to take a hard and critical look at it. Where is your income going? What are you spending it all on every month? Ask yourself if you really need some of those items on your budget or would it be better to cut and save? For example, do you need that Grande from Starbucks every day? Do you need to eat lunch out every day? Where else could you save some money? Do you have larger expenses like a car, student loans or credit card debt? Perhaps it is best to clean those things up while you have a steady income. If you need help setting up a monthly budget, Dave Ramsey's books are simple to understand and cannot be beat. He is wrong in my opinion on the use of other people's money to buy real estate, but if you need to set up a budget and cut expenses, his advice is solid.

The third step is to figure out what amount of income you can live on. After a few months of budgeting and examining your expenses, you should develop a pretty good idea of what your income needs will be. Understand that this number may need to be a bare-bones number to allow you to get you out of your job and get your new business up and running. Understand also that once you start investing full-time, your income will hopefully go up. But let's keep things to a bare minimum for now to be safe.

When figuring out what you will need to live on once you leave your job, you should realize that your budget may change significantly also. For example, you may need to pay for health insurance out of pocket, increasing your costs. On the other hand, gas and dry cleaning bills might be significantly reduced. So you may need to estimate a bit. Estimate high because it is better to be safe. This number you need to live on may be three, four, five or more thousands of dollars per month. Whatever the income number is, be sure it is something that is based in reality because it is very important for the final step towards becoming a full-time investor.

The final step is to determine how you are going to replace your current income to cover what you need to live on. How are you going to put food on your table and pay for health insurance? I decided to use positive cash flow and this is how I calculated what I needed to replace my regular job income. I first figured out that I could buy rental properties, manage them, and make a positive cash flow of approximately $150 per month per unit (I have explained how to do that elsewhere). Through my budget, I determined that I needed about $3,000 a month to cover my basic living expenses. I divided $3,000 by $150 and figured I would need about 20 rental units to replace my current income. The acquisition of cash flowing rental properties then became my goal. By acquiring 20 rental units, I would be able to leave my nine-to-five job.

I acquired my portfolio of properties slowly and steadily while I was still on the job. It took time to learn and grow, and that is likely what you will need to do as well. Your nine-to-five job will at first allow you easier access to other people's money. Plus it will give you something to fall back on if things do not work out. This process did not happen overnight and it will likely not happen that way for you either. In my case, the process from starting to learn about real estate investing to going full-time took **over five years**. Be patient and plan to be in the real estate investing world for the long haul.

That, in a nutshell as they say, is how I became a full-time real estate investor. Your first step is to get your own house in order and figure out where you stand by developing a monthly budget. Then get your real estate income stream started. Being able to leave your job will come with time. Once out, you can begin to set goals to increase your income. Meeting those income goals will be much easier now that you are out and able to focus full-time on growing and expanding your business.

To close this chapter, I want to leave you with some final thoughts for when you finally do quit that job. Never, ever burn any bridges. You really never know what the future holds and you may need those folks again someday. I have been surprised more than once how things always seem to come around again. Also, please make sure your significant other is on board with your goals. If you do not have their support, you are doomed to failure or at the very least a very long and hard road. Lastly, a support network will be really helpful and comforting. That is why communities like your local Real Estate Investors Association can be so important.

How To Manage Your New Found Time

Many newbie investors get into real estate to pursue one dream. That dream of getting out of the rat race and regaining control of their most important asset, their time. That was my dream and I achieved it. You can as well. And believe me, regaining control over your time is a wonderful thing. Interestingly, it can also be one of the biggest challenges you will face. The challenge comes from learning how to manage your newfound time. Gaining control of your time is one thing, learning how to manage it is another.

Have you thought about how you will manage your time when you get it back? You need to. It is so easy to get side tracked when you do not have a boss looking over your shoulder. Plus, getting lost in the daily details is a lot easier than you think. Poor time management is a killer. You can, however take action to preserve your newfound time and keep what you have worked so hard to attain.

The first thing you should do is develop long term business and personal goals. These goals will become a general guide for your newfound time. What types of goals? Your goals could be anything from how big you want your business to be or where you want to live. Take some time now to think about your long term goals. As you move towards becoming a full-time investor, develop and refine those goals. Write them down somewhere so you can see and review them often.

Then, structure each week. Take some time at the beginning of each week to plan it out. Ask yourself what needs to be done to advance towards your goals? What needs to be done each day that week? Are there any deadlines or issues that need immediate attention? What are some regularly scheduled activities that need to be included? It does not matter if you use a fancy spreadsheet, or an app, or just plain old notebook paper for this task, all that matters is that it is done.

Taking the time to develop goals and make a weekly schedule will put you way ahead of most other people, as far as time management goes. Be sure to build some flexibility into your schedule, as one thing I have learned over the years is that the best laid plans can quickly get turned upside down. Leave room for things that will inevitably pop up, both good and bad.

What should you be doing every week? That will depend on your goals and, of course, everyone's goals are and will be different. I think that there are a few items that everyone should be spending some time on each and every week, if not each and every day.

1. **Time Thinking About Your Business** – This is the most important and most overlooked item. You worked so hard on getting out of the rat race, now you have to think about how you are going to stay out. Do this at least once a week. Spend a quiet, undisturbed hour or so where you do nothing but think about your business. What is going on in it? What needs to be changed? How? How can it grow or adapt? What is your competition doing? How can you do it better?

2. **Time For Marketing** – You may not think marketing will have a major role, but marketing is a major part of any successful business. You need to ask yourself the following questions every week. How are you bringing in new business? How are you finding new properties to acquire? How can you keep ahead of your competition? These are all marketing-type questions that you will need to answer to stay on top and grow.

3. **Time Searching For Deals** – You are going to have to knock on some doors, as they say, to acquire properties. Perhaps not literal doors, but in this business, maybe so. When will you scan online databases like the Multiple Listing System? What systems will you put in place to funnel potential deals to you? Who will you network with to find deals? When will you go look at those properties? When will you drive for dollars or recruit new bird dogs? Budget some (a lot, actually)

of your time to focus on these items. Deals also can and do pop up out of nowhere. This is one of the major reasons I advised you to keep some flexibility in your schedule. When a deal appears, you often have to move quickly otherwise it will disappear just as quickly as it popped up. Plan on putting other things aside to get the deal when it pops up.

4. **Time To Meet With Your Spouse/Partner** – If your spouse is also your business partner (and even if they are not), plan a specific time to talk about your business with them. Don't do it at the dinner table or in the evening when everyone is trying to relax. Plan for a specific business meeting.

5. **Time To Get Together With Other Investors** – One of the worst things about being out on your own is that you will not have anyone to commiserate with. If you are still working a full-time job, you may not realize just how important commiseration is. When you are on your own, you will no longer get to hang around the water cooler or later on at the bar with your work buds and talk shop. Talking shop is important. By talking shop you hear about new ideas and it is a form of therapy. One of the best things you can do is join a local real estate club or find a local meetup group. If you cannot find one in your area, form your own. Both finding and forming are easy to do on social media these days. You will find that talking to other investors in the same business will be one of the best things you can do.

6. **Time To Read** – Plan on spending some quiet time reading. Read real estate websites and blogs. Read business journals and trade magazines. Read business books. Reading about your business keeps you informed, provides new insights and can even recharge your batteries. Plus it is quiet. Turn your phone off and the TV off for a little while and read.

7. **Time To Relax and Enjoy** – Do not fill up your entire schedule with real estate. Yes real estate is fun and I understand that you have caught

the bug and now enjoy your work. You need to remember that you got out of the rat race to gain your time back and to enjoy it. So do it! Take some time and plan out all of those things that you wanted to do once you got your time back. Take some more time out to spend on yourself. Go to a matinee movie just because you can. Take your kids to the park. Have a long lunch. Travel. Pick up a new hobby. You can even have absolutely nothing planned. Use your time wisely, but enjoy life as well.

All of the above items matter and are a necessary component of any time management plan. There are two important things to remember however, **be flexible** and **go after the deal**. I know that you wanted to accomplish 'x', 'y' and 'z' today but sometimes life will just throw a wrench in those plans. Things will break, kids will get sick, and fires will arise that you will need to extinguish. Keep space in your schedule for these items as no amount of planning can eliminate them.

Secondly, when a potential deal presents itself you need to drop everything else and go after it. Don't worry about fixing the sink. Don't worry about that tenant. Skip the matinee movie. Getting the deal is often the most important thing we investors do. The really good ones may not come along very often. Go after the potential deal and the payday when they pop up. Someone else will if you do not. Don't put yourself in a position to look back with regret.

Finally, remember that your time is your most valuable asset. Your goal was to get it back. Once you get it back, it must be used wisely or it could disappear. The tips outlined above should help you do just that.

Avoiding Fraud: How To Steer Clear Of Being Taken

We have all heard or read the stories about real estate investors being defrauded. It can happen to anyone and can strike from where you least expect it. Even people you think you can trust can and will commit fraud. To exemplify the point, I can recall a Memphis real estate attorney who was found to be embezzling their clients' money. This attorney was arrested by the FBI, later pled guilty and was sentenced to 20 months in federal prison.

This attorney duped several private lenders into thinking they had made loans on real estate here in Memphis. In reality, the attorney stole the money and used it to purchase beachfront property. This attorney was not some fly-by-night, under the radar attorney. Instead, it was a well known real estate attorney, closing many deals and working with a number of different investors.

I tell this story to both scare and educate you.

Fraud is everywhere and real estate investors can be tempting targets. There is a lot of money being passed around in real estate, thus the impulse to defraud can be great. As real estate investors we must learn and realize that we cannot abdicate our responsibility to keep watch over our own businesses. Unfortunately, that means we have to keep tabs on everyone. Even your attorney could be doing something underhanded as demonstrated by the above story. We simply must know what is happening and where our money is going. Failing to do so just sets you up to get scammed.

I hate to sound so cynical, but it is what it is.

There are concrete things that you can do to make yourself and your business a more difficult target. You can reduce your fraud risk and help ensure that you keep your hard earned money.

How?

Understand What You Are Getting Into – An ignorant and uninformed person is the easiest to defraud. Understanding the deal that you are getting into is a key factor to avoid fraud. Remember that in any real estate deal, the numbers do not lie. The numbers have to be able to be justified. If things cannot be justified then remember the old adage, *if it seems too good to be true, than it probably is.*

Accurate Bookkeeping Is Essential – To know if you have been the victim of fraud you have to know what you had in the first place. How can you know if you have been defrauded if you have no idea how much you are supposed to have or where it is supposed to be? Real estate investors have to keep accurate records. If you use an accountant or bookkeeper, reconcile the work that they are doing every few weeks or so. Do not abdicate your responsibility to your bookkeeper or accountant. You have to stay on top of them.

Keep An Eye On Your Accounts – Keep tabs on *all* of your bank and credit accounts. This could become a daily function as your business grows in size and complexity. Set up your accounts so that notifications are emailed or texted to you in order to immediately catch any large or odd transactions that occur. Check all of your statements for weird and out of place transactions. Immediately follow up on anything that seems suspicious or out of the ordinary. If something seems or feels wrong, check it out. It never hurts to ask, plus it keeps everyone aware that you are staying on top of things.

Get Referrals – I wish that everyone was honest, but it is just not the case. Everyone lives with temptation and everyone can be tempted. Referrals are one of the best ways to weed out the bad apples that can fall to temptation. Discuss your needs with other trusted professionals and investors. What do they have to say? Or even better, what are they not saying? Understand that sometimes silence can say a thousand words.

Do Not Be Too Insular – Look for and seek advice from people outside of a "circle" of connected players. In the story at the beginning of this article, the fraud was aided by the fact that several of the players were inside the same office. They had set up a so called *"one-stop real estate shop"*. You should be cautious of anyone or firm that tries to "keep everything in-house." These people or firms may be completely on the up and up, but insularity can create a wind tunnel effect where you only hear one thing and nothing else. Keeping things too insular is thus a good way to be conned. One-stop shops can be great and hold many advantages, but sometimes it may be best to find and hire your own separate attorney, CPA, appraiser, etc.

Verify Everything – You have to read what you are signing. Do the closing statements match what you were told? Are the amounts correct? Are there any odd charges that you do not understand? Is the money going where it was supposed to? Have your deeds been properly notarized and recorded? Are the notes for the amount you expect and for the property you think it should be for. In today's world mistakes on these documents are most likely to be "copy and paste" errors, but you never know. It is best to review everything just to be sure. Once you sign, you may be on the hook. Again, do not abdicate your responsibility.

Comprehend – Legalese can make your head spin. Big words and long, convoluted paragraphs are a fraudsters dream. You have to make sure that you comprehend what you are signing. Remember that it is *your* money, *your* dreams and *your* head on the line. Do not feel intimidated to sign and do not let yourself be pushed into signing something you do not understand.

Question, Question, Question – Ask lots of questions until you get the answers you need. Fraud hates questions and there is nothing like a probing question or two to expose it. Do not accept non-answers and most definitely do not accept phrases like "it's all covered" or "the computers were down" to your questions. Learn to ask specific, lawyer-like questions that will generate specific answers. Ask who? What? When? Where? And then ask them again if you are not satisfied. If you do not or cannot get the answers you need then stop and go elsewhere.

That Gut Feeling Is There For A Reason – We all know that feeling. Something just feels wrong. We might not be able to explain it, but we can feel it. If something feels wrong, there is likely a reason. We humans are endowed with this sixth sense to help keep us safe. Listen to it. I used the attorney mentioned at the beginning of this chapter once, but I never did again. Both my wife and I just got a bad feeling about things. Nothing I can specifically point my finger at, but sometimes a feeling will be all you have. Listen to what you or your partner's gut is telling you. It might be nothing, or it could save you thousands. It is best to play it safe.

Seek Help – If you are the victim of fraud do not put your head in the sand. That is what the fraudsters are hoping you will do. Call the authorities and file a complaint. Hopefully, they will start an investigation and take action. Remember, **fraud is not your fault.** You are the victim and you should be mad. At the very least learn from your experience and take steps to try and prevent a recurrence in the future.

Despite all of the rules, regulations and laws out there, it is ultimately up to us as investors to be on guard for fraud. Caveat emptor (let the buyer beware) is still a good rule to live by. The police are great at documenting crimes, but not so great at preventing them. It will be all up to you. Do not let greed or ambition blind you. If something feels wrong, it likely is. Things will happen and you may make a mistake by trusting the wrong

135

person. If you do, learn from it. Move forward and do not let it scare you away and keep you out of the business.

Let me close by saying that if you become aware of any type of questionable dealings you should move on and leave them behind. The quick buck may be tempting but you are and will be judged by the company you keep. We real estate investors often all know each other as the real estate investing world can be pretty tight-knit. We are aware of reputations. You only have one reputation, do not tarnish it.

The Biggest Problem Real Estate Investors Have

Our local real estate investors association often brings in speakers from around the country to deliver presentations on various topics. Following one of those meetings, several of us investors got together with the guest speaker for some food, drinks and conversation. It can be very interesting to talk with these guest speakers since they travel all over the country and can thus have perspectives that can and do differ greatly from your own, local insights.

As the conversation turned I asked our guest what, in their opinion, is the biggest problem most real estate investors have. Without blinking or giving it another thought our guest said "The biggest problem is that most folks do not run their investments as a business, but rather as a hobby. In doing so, they work *in* rather than *on* their business".

Many newbies, myself included when I was starting out, make the mistake of thinking that they can do it all themselves. They think that they can save money by doing repairs or cutting grass. The reality is, they can't do it all themselves and they really are not saving money. They are in fact losing money. Many newbies fail to realize or think about all of the costs they are incurring by trying to do it all themselves and working **in** their business.

As an investor, your number one job is to make money. You cannot do that if you are painting a wall, fixing the plumbing, cutting the grass, running to the bank, putting stamps on envelopes or whatever. Yes, you have to spend money to get others to do those jobs, but by doing so it will free up your time so you can go out there and make the money to pay them plus a lot more.

Think about it. If you are repairing the kitchen sink, when will you have time to put together a marketing program to find deals? If you are painting a wall, when do you have time to go out and look at and analyze potential properties? The answer is you will not have the time and those potential deals will be lost to others.

If you try to do everything yourself, I can tell you that you will also quickly burn out. You will begin to hate real estate investing and wish you had your old life back. I don't want that to happen to you.

You, as the real estate investor and business owner, have to realize that you cannot and should not do it all. You have to **let things go** in order to grow. Honestly, this is one of the hardest lessons to learn. After all, no one will do it like you. That may be true, but Sam Walton of Walmart, Jeff Bezos of Amazon or Mark Zuckerberg of Facebook did not get where they are by acting alone. They let things go by hiring others to help them. You will also have to hire competent people to help you out.

Work *on* your business not *in* it. Hire contractors to paint the walls and cut the grass. Hire an assistant to run to the bank and mail out the bills. Remember, your job is to grow your business, not get stuck in it.

Should You Incorporate Right Away?

Every year when I look over my taxes, I think about the corporations I have set up. When I started out, before I even bought a property, I set up an LLC to hold my rentals. Later, I set up a chapter S corporation for property management and another LLC for my retail property flipping business, so I am no stranger to corporate structures.

I can recall many years ago being at a real estate seminar listening to one of the expert gurus talking about how you had to incorporate before you did anything else to protect your anonymity and your assets. I am sure many of you have read or heard the same thing. Is that advice correct? Should you incorporate right away? With hindsight, I can now look back and answer that question. What's more, I can tell you if incorporating my business was worth it. Did the costs of incorporating outweigh the benefits?

Before answering I want to make a few things clear. I want to go through the pros and cons to incorporation. By doing so, you will better understand why I have the answer I do.

The Pros

Appearance is sometimes everything and incorporation has helped my business appearance in two ways. First, incorporation made my business appear more legitimate. People just feel more comfortable when they see that LLC. In reality, incorporation has nothing to do with legitimacy, it is only perception. But, perception is often reality.

Secondly, incorporation made our business appear more professional. Of course the reason we appear professional is because of how we run our business, but over the years banks and others have appreciated the fact that we run our businesses within a corporate structure. We received this appreciation even though we could not find a bank that would make a loan to our newly formed LLC. Nor will you. Banks like LLC's to be "seasoned" for at least two years. It is a weird catch-22 for the investor. People like to see the LLC structure, but they will often not do business with it until it has seasoned.

Corporate structures also provide a good bit of asset and liability protection. The LLC and S corporation structures (C corporations are not something you will generally utilize in real estate investing due to tax consequences) are completely separate entities from their shareholders (you). It is as if they are completely different people. This fact does provide a liability shield between our business and personal lives. This liability shield is perhaps the main benefit of incorporating and the main reason that people are advised to do it. It puts some space between your business and personal assets in case you are ever sued. We do live in a society that seems to run on lawsuits, so some form of asset and liability protection is a necessity, especially as your business grows.

There is a bit of anonymity that comes with incorporation. Technology has almost ended this benefit as a few properly placed clicks on the internet will often lift that curtain of anonymity. True anonymity can be achieved, but it comes with increased levels of complication and costs.

The Cons

Very few things in life are free and corporate entities are not one of them. Corporate entities cost money to maintain. This money is in the form of taxes and fees. Every state has some amount of annual filing fees, and if your entity does business in another state, there are likely more fees piled on top of that. Taxes are also often an additional cost. Tennessee, where I am located, has franchise and excise taxes, for example. These taxes can make incorporation not worth the cost. Other states may have these or other types of taxes on corporate structures as well.

In addition to the monetary costs, the entities also cost time. Everything about corporate entities has a piece of paper attached to it. There are annual meetings and corporate minutes, bank accounts and receipts, tax forms and annual reports. All of this paperwork means more time sucked away from you in order to keep everything together. Not keeping everything together may mean that your protective corporate asset shield can be easily pierced.

Finally, everything is more complicated. When you have and are using corporate entities, you cannot commingle anything. You have to be sure that everything is kept separate and what belongs to one entity is not placed in, or commingled with, what belongs to another, including the entity of yourself. In other words you have to keep separate bank accounts and records for each entity. Funds cannot generally cross the boundaries between those accounts. You also have to remember who you are when signing documents. Are you signing for something personally or as the officer of your LLC? Mistakes here can cost you plenty.

The Answer – Should You Incorporate Right Away?

So, was the guru correct? Was incorporating right away a necessity? No, it was not, especially when starting out. I suggest getting into the business first to see if it is right for you and then add in the corporate complications later if you wish. In fact, I am not sure incorporating is necessary at all. Over the years I have met numerous investors who have never incorporated and they have done just fine. There are other investors I know who have even de-incorporated due to tax consequences. LLCs and other entities certainly have their place, but you can do just fine without them. The time and costs needed to keep up with everything is not always trivial. They are real and something you need to consider. It all comes down to what is going to let you be able to sleep at night, and that is something only you can judge. I hope these insights will help you decide.

141

Would I Do It Again?

Most likely I would, just perhaps not at first. I do like the liability protection and the benefits of looking more professional. I believe I can say that looking more professional has truly benefited our business.

Section 5 – Going Forward As A Full-time Real Estate Investor

Real estate investing will be a fun and exciting venture. You are going to learn a lot about yourself, about business and about other people. It does, however, come with some new realities and perceptions. Some of these you may expect. Some you may not.

Life is different when you are out on your own. At times you will feel like you are on top of the world. Other times you will feel isolated and alone. It can at times feel like the whole world is working against you. It can also leave you with a wonderful feeling of success and satisfaction.

This chapter is about some of those new realities and perceptions you might experience. I share them here in hopes you will find the content insightful and helpful as you continue to move forward as a real estate investor.

How To Stay Afloat When You Feel You Are Being Pulled Under

Being a real estate investor means that you are often going to be pushed beyond what you are comfortable with. It has to. It is an ever-changing business with new people, properties and opportunities coming our way all the time. These people, properties and opportunities can at times be uplifting and fulfilling. At other times though, these things can really drag us down by being challenging, dishonest, intimidating, disheartening, ignorant, stubborn, or a whole host of other adjectives. Pile a few of those downers on top of each other in one day and then let a few of those days begin to stack up and it can be enough to make even the most experienced investor feel like they are being pulled under. I know because I have felt like I was being pulled under more than once and unfortunately, you will likely feel it too at some point.

But, I am still here and I am doing pretty well. I am still here because there are things I did to keep my head above water. There are ways to get back to the beach when it feels like the tide is pulling you out.

Breathe – Yes, the simple act of breathing can do a lot. One of the first things you must do when you feel you are being pulled under is to stop, step back, take a moment and breathe deeply. This simple act can reduce your stress and clear you mind. And a clear mind is what you need to move forward.

Show Confidence – You need to act like you are supposed to be where you are, even if you do not feel like you should be. In effect, you need to *fake it until you make it*. If you feel and demonstrate confidence, studies show that it **will** actually change your brain chemistry and actually make you more confident. Just feeling confident will actually build your confidence. It will also change how everyone around you acts. They will not know what is really going on in your head (which might be the overwhelming urge to run away!). They only know what they see. People respect a confident person. Take a minute and breathe. Project a positive and confident body posture. Remember that you are the investor and you are likely calling the shots. It is your property. It is your deal. You make the decisions. Act like it! Showing confidence may take a little practice, but even if conjured, it will pull you up and out of the water.

Seek Help – There is nothing new under the sun. Whatever it is that you are experiencing, it is not something that another investor has not experienced and dealt with before. Thus, there is no reason you need to feel like you are going into anything alone. You can and should ask for help and advice from other real estate investors. The best in any business became the best by asking for help. You should too. Where can you ask for help? You can ask me at my blog. If not me and my blog, there are forums and groups all over the internet with people happy to help you. If you happen to live in a larger city, I bet that there are investor groups that meet all the time. I know of at least a dozen real estate investor meetings here in the Memphis area that I could go to every month. Do not think you need to go this route alone, and do not think that there is any problem that cannot be figured out. Get out there and ask for help. If you do, in time I bet you will be the one that others are seeking help from in the future.

Educate Yourself – Do you know what most people are afraid of? It is the unknown. We fear what we do not know. Real estate investing due to its very nature is going to be filled with unknowns. There are sellers you have never met. Neighborhoods you have never been in and repairs that you have never encountered. You know what will take away that fear? Knowledge. Nothing takes away fear and anxiety like a little knowledge, and knowledge is easy to find and easy to get. Do you have an unexpected maintenance issue? Ask the hive mind of the internet what to do and get some contractor quotes. Need to learn how to keep more accurate books?

147

I bet there is a YouTube video to tell you how. It is so easy to get good information these days. Take advantage of it.

Keep Calm And Carry On – Another cliché, but those British signs from World War II were correct. So, keep calm and carry on. Some of the worst decisions I have ever made were when I lost my cool and got angry or upset. If things are getting a bit out of control the first thing to do is to realize it and remove yourself from whatever the situation is that is affecting you. Go somewhere else, breathe and calm down, especially if you need to make any type of decision. Otherwise, you may do something rash or unwise that you may regret later and only add to your stress.

Recall That You Have Faced Adversity Before – Adversity happens all the time. It is part of life. You have been through adversity before and survived. This time the situation may be different, but the adversity you feel is the same. It may have been hard, but you made it. Things may seem insurmountable or overwhelming when they are occurring right in front of you, but later on we often look back at these things and laugh. Remember that one day you will probably be laughing at whatever the current adverse situation is as well.

What Does Not Kill You Will Make You Stronger – The clichés keep coming but sometimes we all need to be reminded of them. Over the years, I have been through some serious issues. I have had properties burn down. I have lost out on deals and gotten into things I was sure I would never get out of. I have been screamed at by tenants and I have angered property owners (Why did I get into real estate again?). But I am still here and all of those experiences have made me a stronger and a better real estate investor and person. The same thing will happen to you if you stick with it.

Realize That You Are In Control – You may not feel like it, but you are in control. You are working the deal. You are working on your business. It is your property and it is your life. You have the control and ability to choose to work the deal or not. You can control who you work with. You do not have to work with jerks or idiots. In fact, I do not recommend it. If someone is a jerk or acting like a fool, leave them behind and move one. You do not need them, their drama or their deals in your life.

Everyone Else Likely Feels The Same Way You Do – Very few people actually have their lives put together perfectly. Most people will feel just like you do. They are scared and intimidated at meeting new people and trying to work the deal. They fear rejection, the unknown and failure. They want the same things and have the same goals as you do. They are human too. Keep this fact in mind as you go through this business. I have found over the years that going into any situation with the goal to help or create a "win/win" situation really makes things a lot easier. Helping others and solving problems is the key to success in this business and that starts with understanding that the other person is just as overwhelmed as you are. Be kind and supportive.

Learn To Say No – You cannot take on everything nor can you make everyone happy. Learning to say no will go a long way towards keeping you sane and from feeling like you are going under. For some this can be hard to do, but you must learn. Not every deal is for you. Nor do you need everyone in your life. Learn to say no. Learn to say no a lot.

The above may seem difficult, but if you give these ideas a try, being a real estate investor will get easier and easier for you. You are not alone as a newbie real estate investor. We have all been where you are and we are now better off for it. Does it get easier as you go forward? Yes. There will come a time when you will not need to fake it anymore. Do the challenges ever stop? No, they do not. It is just a part of the real estate investing business. It is I guess, in some strange way, a part of what makes this business so great and so fun.

Be Thankful

Are you thankful that you have found real estate investing yet? If you are not, you should take a little time to reflect. With experience, I can now look back over my real estate investing career and see all of the things that real estate investing has provided or allowed me to do. Financially, things have gone well, but there are other elements that I am thankful for, elements that are a bit more important to me than money. Hopefully you will be thankful for these same elements one day as well.

I Got My Time Back – This has got to be my number one item that I am thankful for. I have my time to do with as I please. I no longer have a "full-time" job. I no longer have to commute or ask for a day off. My time is my own to do with as I please. I can work on my business or not. I can write this book or not. I have a lot more time for all of the things that I like to do, which of course includes the fun of investing in real estate.

I Have Learned Confidence – I can negotiate with ease. I can confidently talk business with a banker and direct a host of contractors on a large rehab job. I can also hang a door, do minor carpentry, run numbers, build websites and a host of other things. I cannot even begin to count all of the new skills that I have learned. Learning these things has provided me with a confidence that I simply did not have before. I am especially thankful for that.

I Have Made A Lot Of New Friends – I have met a lot of different people because I became a real estate investor. Many have become my good friends. I would likely never have met these people if it was not for real estate investing. One of the friends I have made is fond of saying that all of his friends are also his competitors. We investors appreciate other investors. We appreciate our competition. There are very few fields out there that can really say that, but real estate investing is one of them. The friends I have made are great additions to my life and I am very thankful to have met them.

I Have Become Well Rounded – Real estate investing exposed me to many new ideas and concepts that I would likely never have been exposed to otherwise It has allowed me to think of new ways of doing things and taken my education and knowledge to levels that I do not believe I could have achieved with anything else. My interaction with my new friends that I discussed above has pointed me in directions and led to discussions I never would have had before. My mind has truly been expanded and for that I am thankful.

I Am A Better Person – Because real estate investing forced me to try things I never would have tried before and because it forced me to move beyond where I felt safe and comfortable, I believe real estate investing has made me a better person. For one, I do not think that I would ever have thought of writing a blog and a book before taking this great adventure. I have also had experiences that might not have happened. Real estate has opened my eyes to how the world works and how other people live. While those experiences were at times infuriating they also provided sympathy, understanding and were also humbling.

So yes, I am very thankful that I got into real estate investing. You may not feel very thankful yet, but give it time. Eventually you, too, will be very thankful for all that real estate investing provides.

Dealing With The Pervasive Anti-Landlord Mentality

When you become a landlord, I can almost guarantee that you will someday find yourself in the following situation. You will be making small talk in some social gathering and someone will ask, "What do you do?" Being proud of what you do and what you have accomplished you will tell them that you are a landlord. Very often the next thing out of their mouth is something along the lines of, "Oh, you're a slumlord."

If you have not found yourself in this situation, wait for it, it will happen. It is such a natural reaction for some people and it has happened to me too many times for it to just be a coincidence. This line of slumlord thinking is so pervasive that I began to wonder where it comes from and why it is so prevalent. Why do so many think that all landlords are slumlords? Why will people assume that you and I are one? What is this anti-landlord mentality and where does it come from?

Perhaps it is all a misunderstanding. People who are not landlords simply do not understand what the business involves. They do not realize how difficult it is to maintain properties and deal with tenants.

These misunderstandings mean there could be a lot of ignorance involved. No, I do not mean that the people throwing around the slumlord moniker are stupid. Instead I mean that these people are not aware of just how much is involved in running your own real estate investment business. We have to remember that most have no idea what it takes to run a successful business because they simply have no experience. This just makes them ignorant of what it takes.

Of course there could be other reasons. One is disdain. Some people do not like money or the thought of others making it. They think that anyone making money is somehow exploiting others, when nothing could be further from the truth.

People can also be resentful. Perhaps they tried to start their own business and failed. Perhaps they had a bad landlord experience in the past. Perhaps they are not as successful as they want to be and are trying to blame anyone other than themselves. They do not like your success because it reflects poorly on them. It is a natural but unfortunate human response.

Finally, I think there could be some envy involved. Envy is another completely natural human response that can be very difficult to control. People are simply going to be envious of what you have created and what you have accomplished. Envy often leads to hate and intolerance. It is not listed as one of the seven deadly sins without reason.

Whatever the reason for someone calling me a slumlord, I always work hard to keep my calm and see the experience as a teaching moment. I will generally try and respond with something like the following. "No, I'm not a slumlord. I work hard to provide decent housing at a reasonable price. I do that while providing jobs, paying taxes and making my city a better place."

That is usually enough to either shut them up or better yet, get a conversation going.

As I said, I often view these as teaching moments and thus I actually hope to get a conversation going. I want to talk to people with this attitude. I want to talk to them about how hard it can be to maintain properties. I want to tell them about my tenant horror stories. I want to tell them about the property that burned down, about fighting with city hall and about all of the "seminars" that I have taken. I want them to understand that often there is not much left over at the end of the month after everyone has reached into my pocket and taken their share.

I want to help people understand just how difficult running a business is. If they want to listen, I will tell them how I got started and explain how they could as well. Depending on the situation, I might even discuss how they could become an investor with our company and make some money along with us. Some people are eager to listen and learn and I can tell they soon feel regrets about their remarks. Some will never get it, no matter how hard you try. They are just too entrenched with their envy, their disdain and their beliefs.

I can almost guarantee that once you have a bit of success, you will have to face and deal with the anti-landlord mentality. Prepare yourself to not only hear it from new people that you meet and interact with, but also from people you have known for a while. Use the opportunity to try and educate. Do not get mad and belittle, that will serve to only reinforce the mentality. Killing them with kindness is always the best policy.

You Are No Longer Normal

Many things in life get easier the more that you do them. In some ways, real estate investing does get easier the more that you do. It becomes more familiar. You grow a thicker skin and become wiser. In other ways real estate investing gets harder. After 15 years as a real estate investor, there are still some things that I thought would get easier but never did. And I think a lot of that is due to the fact that real estate investors are cut from a different mold. We do not resemble, act or think like the majority who work in the nine-to-five world. Our business is also unconventional and unlike most other businesses out there. Basically, we real estate investors are no longer "normal," whatever "normal" is.

And that is the thing. The world is not made for us or our unconventional nature. The world is made for those who have the nine-to-five jobs. It is made for people whose real estate experience ends with the ownership of their own home. The world has a very narrowly defined perspective and once you are outside of this perspective you become something that many cannot understand. Something many do not even want to try to understand. You become something that is just not normal.

You see, real estate investing is simply not something that the normal person does or even understands. Most people do not own a bunch of properties, and not having nine-to-five income is almost unheard of. You and I understand that real estate can and does tend to work out very well, but many others not familiar with what we do will see you as strange and as a risk.

This unfounded perception of risk unfortunately will lay the ground for many speed bumps as you travel along the real estate investing road. Funding may dry up as financial institutions once happy to lend now see you as a risk because you have "too many properties." These institutions cannot fathom how you will ever be able to pay them back if you do not have a "real" job. It is almost like they have never ever heard of rental income.

The same thing may happen with your long-term insurance company. The company that once told you that you were in good hands will now tell you to take a hike. Almost overnight they can decide that you are too much of a risk and drop your coverage, leaving you scrambling to find another carrier. Your newfound unconventional nature is not seen as a good thing, it is seen as a risk. It is not normal.

Be prepared to not be normal anymore. Be ready to become unconventional, to be outside of others realm of experience and world view. It can hit you hard and be a significant challenge to you as you try to go forward. I, for example, have been dropped by several insurance companies for no apparent reason, once even before I closed on the property. I once had a loan processor at a major bank inform me he could not process my refinance application simply because he did not have enough slots for all of my property addresses on his application form. Incredible, but you see what I mean. I was not normal anymore. They simply did not know how to process me anymore and I was out. I survived and you will as well. It is all part of the fun of being a real estate investor.

For good or bad, humans have organized and categorized almost everything in various easily recognizable compartments. In a lot of ways this categorization is good because organization is good. It also can really hinder us because our unconventional nature means that we will not neatly fit into these categories anymore. It can be a real problem as you try to move forward and achieve your real estate investing goals. This problem is not insurmountable. It is just something that you are going to have to recognize and deal with. It is something that you are going to have to work at and get creative to solve.

We fellow real estate investors realize that you must be doing something right, even if everyone else does not. Your fellow real estate investors have all "been there and done that" and there is nothing new about it when it happens to you. We all survived and turned out better for it. You will as well.

Good luck! Thanks for reading and happy investing!

Please let me know what you thought of this book by clicking here to leave a review on Amazon. Also, let me know how you are doing. Go to my blog Smarterlandlording.com and connect with me there.

About Kevin Perk

I come from a background with little real estate or business experience. Growing up, my family did not own any real estate except for our home. My dad, a hard worker, was employed with the federal government all of his adult life, while mom stayed home to take care of me. We once tried to run my uncle's grocery store when he got sick but became quickly overwhelmed and the business was sold. In short, as far as the business world was concerned, I only knew about the nine-to-five jobs that my dad and nearly everyone around me had.

Thus, I believed that the correct path to follow in life was the typical one. Go to school while working a part-time job (McDonald's for me). Go to college and get a degree, and then get a full-time job just like my dad had done. So, that is just what I did. However, once I got to that full-time job the reality of my situation set in (better late than never I guess). I realized that I was going to have to do that job for the next 30 or so years. And while I liked many aspects of my job and most of the people I worked with, I knew there had to be something better. I just did not know where to look.

Finally, one night my wife was watching a fundraiser on the local PBS station. I was out on the porch and she called me inside. "This guy is making a lot of sense" she said. "You should watch this." That guy was Robert Kiyosaki and watch I did. He was making a lot of sense

That was over 15 years ago and I have never looked back. Since that time I have become a real estate investor, bought and sold many properties and quit my nine-to-five job. I have been "retired" and a full-time investor now for over a dozen years.

I hope I can be that person who makes a lot of sense to you like Kiyosaki did to me. While I am not on PBS, I am trying to spread the word with this book and my blog, Smarterlandlording.com. Real estate investing gave me my life back. I no longer commute or punch a time clock. I no longer have to be anywhere I do not want to be. Real estate investing has provided me with everything I want and more, and it can for you too.

Made in the USA
Lexington, KY
27 September 2019